MINIATURE GARDENS

Some of the material in this book has been revised from my earlier books, but as these are now all out of print, I have woven what seems to me the best and the most useful from each of them and then added much that I have learned, by my own experience, over the years since they were published.

Miniature Gardens

ANNE ASHBERRY

illustrated by
Creina Glegg

DA·VID & CHARLES
NEWTON ABBOT   LONDON
NORTH POMFRET (VT)   VANCOUVER

ISBN 0 7153 7289 0
Library of Congress Catalog Card Number 76–54085

Set in 11 on 13pt Times
by Trade Linotype Limited Birmingham
and printed in Great Britain
by Biddles Limited Guildford
for David & Charles (Publishers) Limited
Brunel House   Newton Abbot   Devon

Published in the United States of America
by David & Charles Inc
North Pomfret   Vermont 05053   USA

Published in Canada
by Douglas David & Charles Limited
1875 Welch Street   North Vancouver   BC

CONTENTS

All the gardens illustrated in this book have been designed by the author

INTRODUCTION

Many people find happiness, as well as relief from anxieties, in growing plants, for gardening is one of the few pleasures which can be enjoyed either alone or with companions. Some would-be gardeners are thwarted, either by lack of space or physical disability, so cannot garden in the usual way. For them a trough garden, raised up to a convenient height, planted with *natural* miniature trees, tiny shrubs, roses and other plants in proportion, can create a landscape in miniature, opening a new world of beauty and interest.

Apart from those who are deprived of normal gardening there are many who have gardens, large or small, but cannot resist the miniature trees and plants, which have an enchantment of their own. These can only be appreciated if raised well above ground level, so that they can be observed and enjoyed in all their exquisite detail.

'How did you start making these gardens?' is a question often put to me. The answer is that this idea developed from three window gardens which I made many years ago to satisfy my own desperate need to grow plants when I was living in a London flat. Frequently, I stayed with friends who had lovely gardens, (one in particular included a wonderful rock garden). I was fascinated by a group of tiny conifers which, although they were only a small part of the rock garden, were in themselves a complete scene.

Back in my flat I often thought longingly of them. Suddenly I had the idea—which now seems so simple and so obvious, but had not occurred to me, or anyone else—that a group of carefully selected miniature trees and plants, arranged in a definite design, would make what I wanted so badly, a real garden, small enough to have on a window-ledge. I planned to have three of these to suit a bay window, with the boxes shallow so that the top of the containers would be level with the base of the windows. Most window-boxes are 6in to 8in deep and seen from within the room there is a vast expanse of wood or plastic; whereas with my shallow boxes there was very little of them visible above the window-frame, so the trees and the plants, which do not need more than 4in depth of soil, were shown to full advantage.

These three little gardens gave me and my friends so much pleasure that I thought there must be many other flat-dwellers who, like myself, yearned for a garden. So the scheme of making landscapes in miniature for other people's window-ledges or balconies, shaped itself in my mind. I decided to specialise in gardens for town-dwellers and my first step was to visit as many nurseries as possible to assess what I could acquire for a potential stock of suitable trees and plants. My own three gardens were furnished with gifts from friends and I did not know what scope there would be, but soon found that I would have to be selective. Some nurseries had a wide range of rock plants, but only a few of the smaller alpines. Others had a stock of rarities which were not suitable for the amateur, whilst one or two nurseries specialised in what were classed as 'dwarf conifers'; amongst the latter there were not many which were really slow-growing enough to be used in small gardens for, although classed as 'dwarf', they would soon outgrow a window garden.

Of course I made mistakes, sometimes misled by a young pot plant with a small flower, which proved to be an invasive rock plant, far too rampant for a window garden. Later on, two most understanding nurserymen agreed to grow some plants especially for my work, when I had proved to myself which species were most successful in the rather special conditions. It was very many years before I was able to have a place in the country in which to grow the plants myself; this not only increased my pleasure in the work, but enabled me to supply a wider range of trees and plants.

In between the times when I was on these tours of discovery I was also studying the requirements of the trees and plants which seemed the most suitable, and planning how garden design could be adapted to the rather special and limited conditions, always bearing in mind the importance of balance and proportion. My scheme was to have gardens of varying sizes and designs to be on show and, in between studying these problems, I was searching for a place where I could make and exhibit the gardens. At last I found one in Kensington and launched out on this adventure.

My first display aroused considerable interest and had some publicity in the Press. Although many people who had no gardens were happy to have miniature landscapes for their window-ledges or balconies, to my surprise and pleasure I was soon asked to design and plant trough gardens for people who had large gardens—either in town or the country—but found the charm of the miniature trees and plants quite irresistible.

My first book was published in 1951 and brought me many friends, of whom Creina Glegg had the greatest effect on my life and work. She came to help in the nursery and later on became my partner. Subsequently, we worked together on five different books, which she illustrated. This is the sixth, based on our joint experience of growing miniature trees and plants. Over the years our powers of observation and appreciation of their beauty has increased and we both hope that friends old and new will find pleasure in these pages.

Advantages of Miniature Gardens

True gardens in miniature appeal to people of all ages, from the very young to the elderly, especially if the latter have been keen gardeners; to the sick and the healthy and also to those of all walks of life, from doctors, nurses, accountants, engineers, prison visitors and coal miners to Royalty. There are some from these very different groups who have one thing in common, a great love of growing plants and an appreciation of beauty in miniature.

Raised well above ground-level a complete well-designed landscape—whether a formal garden, a woodland scene or a rock garden in miniature—will give the impression of a large garden seen through the wrong end of a telescope; although the view is reduced in size, the details of the trees and plants can be seen more clearly than if grown at ground-level. If carefully selected with approximately the same rate of growth, the trees and plants remain well-proportioned in leaf, bud and flower.

Several elderly gardeners, whose eyesight is failing, have expressed their pleasure in a raised garden which enables them to see the plants more clearly and enjoy the wonderful beauty of their design on such a small scale. One example of this is *Cassiope mertensiana*. If seen from above when in flower it is just a scattering of white bells; if seen in profile the structure of the branchlets, the minute whipcord leaves with erect reddish flower-stems rising about 1in above the foliage and then bending over to suspend the pendulous, pure-white bell flowers each with a calyx of bronze red, shows a plant of exquisite beauty, which might well be overlooked if grown close to the ground.

Most of the miniature plants, usually known as alpines, are natives of mountainous districts in different parts of the world, from China and Tibet, the American Rockies, the Swiss Alps, the Pyrenees, Greece and Italy to the Middle East, Australia and New Zealand. Two of the main factors which cause the plants to develop the low compact habit of growth, which is so enchanting, are the exposed conditions (where no tall plant could survive) and the intense light at high altitudes for as shade induces tall growth, so light has the reverse effect. It should be emphasised that the plants described in this book are truly miniature in leaf, bud and flower, but there are some alpine plants which, although growing close to the ground, have fairly large leaves and flowers, so are not suitable subjects for a miniature garden.

In their native habitat many alpine plants have a period submerged beneath a blanket of snow which protects them from frost and icy winds; but most of them will, if given suitable conditions, grow well in the lowlands where any snow is of short duration. These plants need an open position, good drainage and a porous soil; if grown in rich soil they tend to develop lush foliage and poor flowers, or no flowers at all. Too much shade sometimes produces the same effect.

The usual reaction of people who see these miniatures for the first time is to marvel that any plant so minute, so exquisitely proportioned and apparently so delicate, is really quite hardy. Other people who are familiar with some of these plants grown in the rock garden, usually in groups to show a mass of colour, do not always appreciate their individual charm, for to see the almost ethereal beauty of their form and colour it is essential to bring them to a level where they can be closely observed and enjoyed.

Most of the miniature trees are evergreen conifers, but there are a few deciduous species. The conifers are the most important feature of the garden, giving height and proportion to the little landscape. Their colours and decorative shapes make them indispensable. Unlike the plants mentioned above they are not all alpines, but their origin and descriptions will be dealt with in a later chapter.

Apart from the trees and alpines there are some enchanting little shrubs and bulbs, also natives of mountainous districts, most of which flower in the early spring. Many of the plants are minute replicas of familiar garden flowers such as dianthus, primulas, campanulas, violets and irises. There are also others, which have no full-scale counterparts, with a unique charm of their own, erinus, soldanella, saxifraga, gentian and many others which flower generously and grow in harmony with the trees and plants mentioned above. Most of the miniature roses are hybrids; there are varieties of pink, white, yellow and red.

As there are so few alpines which are a true red, the latter add valuable colour to the garden.

The popular interest in bonsai—imported trees from Japan, which have been artificially stunted and have an almost imperceptible rate of growth—has created a strange fallacy that *natural* miniature trees and plants do not grow. Some of these trees will increase in height and spread—the rate of growth varies considerably according to the different species—and the alpines, although they do not increase in stature, will spread and need cutting back or dividing.

When I first started making these miniature gardens my idea was to create, as near as possible, miniature replicas of gardens of the Western world, quite distinct from Japanese gardens. For the first few years visitors to any exhibition where my gardens were displayed, or to the Nursery, would tell me didactically that they were Japanese, because it was a popular fallacy that all miniature trees and plants must be Japanese.

Whilst it is true that many of the conifers, acers and a few of the smallest alpines (such as *Viola yakusimana*) were natives of Japan, the traditional Japanese gardens are nothing like those described in this book. Japanese gardens are constructed with conifers, rock and water, with very few, if any, flowering plants. Each stone or rock is selected for its shape, and has a name and meaning. Their arrangement in connection with the water has a definite significance. A few ornaments, a bridge or a stone lantern may be part of the design.

Such gardens are very beautiful indeed, especially those of a rare and artistic restraint and there are many books on the subject, but this book deals with an entirely different aspect of gardening – the creation of gardens in the occidental style – quite different from the oriental.

One great advantage of miniature gardening is that many of the tiny plants, especially the daffodils, will come into flower much earlier than their full-scale relatives, so giving colour and interest when most large garden plants are dormant. One of the earliest is a small trumpet daffodil, *Narcissus asturiensis,* which blooms in December and January. Also, in winter the evergreen conifers have a subtle change of colour, whilst the deciduous shrubs (acers, salix and zelkovas) have a beauty of structure which is clearly defined when their branches are bare of foliage, followed by the emergence of the minute new leaves in the spring.

In *The English Rock Garden,* written in 1913, Reginald Farrer wrote ' . . . but a little garden, the littler the better, is your richest chance of happiness and success'. Now, over sixty years later, this is even more true for in these troubled times when disasters and horrors of greater magnitude seem to grow more commonplace and we are saturated with reports of horrors which are almost beyond human understanding, it is refreshing to realise that trees and plants go on growing; they have no politics, no loud voices and, whatever else is happening, one can still enjoy the tranquil beauty of these little trees and plants, even if only in a small trough on a window ledge. For, to watch them develop, putting forth their minute new growth of leaf, bud and then flower in their natural seasons is a solace and a source of endless enrichment.

1

POSITION FOR A MINIATURE GARDEN

For anyone who has a garden and wishes to add a trough garden on a pedestal, there is usually a fairly wide choice of positions for this. It could be the centre-piece on a terrace or lawn; a popular place is quite near the house, fairly close to a window where the little garden can be seen and enjoyed from within on a winter's day. In a small town garden with a paved courtyard, one or more trough gardens, also raised up on pedestals, can transform the dullest area into a place of delight.

Most of the plants, especially the trees and shrubs, will tolerate, or even enjoy, a little shade if the garden is in a position where the shade is cast by a large tree, but the garden is not directly below it. In the latter position, the trough garden may be covered with wet and decaying leaves in the autumn – even evergreen conifers shed some leaves – and also subjected to drips from the branches. The wet leaves spoil the look of the garden, robbing the low-growing plants of light and air and also encourage slugs and woodlice; whilst continuous drips from the branches above will make holes or channels in the soil, sometimes exposing some of the roots. If such an undesirable position is unavoidable, then it will be necessary to protect the garden as much as possible by removing the fallen leaves and filling in any holes or channels with coarse soil, mostly sand or chippings.

To flat-dwellers who have no space at all for a trough garden on a pedestal, a window garden is the only alternative. Some old houses have very wide window-ledges and these present no difficulties; tapered wedges keep the garden horizontal by compensating for the slope of the window-ledge, which is so constructed to allow rain to drain away. In some modern buildings the window-ledges are so narrow that they cannot support a trough. This can be overcome by having sturdy brackets fixed to the wall, projecting beyond the window-ledge.

In some cases a would-be gardener has no space and no window-ledge and is not allowed by the landlord to put up the brackets as described above. One such frustrated gardener who was passionately anxious to have a miniature garden, lived in a mews cottage which had no window-ledges. Some of her neighbours had tubs either side of their front doors, but in her case these positions were occupied by metal cupboards, one to conceal the dustbin and the other to contain coal. She had the brilliant idea of having a shallow concrete trough made to rest on the top of each cupboard. They were about 30in square and 3in deep, and enabled her to have a rock garden on one side of the door and a miniature rose garden on the other. These two gardens not only gave her very great pleasure, combined with a sense of triumph, but they also fascinated both the dustmen and the coalmen, as well as her neighbours.

Balcony gardens, like those for a window-ledge, can be planted in shallow containers. Usually such a garden is more exposed than one on a window-ledge and should get more direct light, which allows for a wider selection of plants. If the balcony is spacious enough it can have a series of long narrow troughs, making one complete landscape or a series of different designs. In some cases the size of the balcony limits the scheme to only one trough. There are many balconies where the railings are made of wrought iron, in which case the trough must be supported by sturdy angle-brackets securely fastened to take the weight of the trough, or the troughs could stand on individual pedestals. Many modern balconies have concrete parapets which can support a narrow trough garden. For one extensive balcony which went the full length of the house and

Fig 1

was accessible from three pairs of French windows, I designed a series of gardens in troughs 12in wide which rested on the concrete parapet (fig 1). Each garden was planned to be viewed from inside the French windows as an individual garden; but the whole viewed from the street was one continuous landscape.

One word of warning should be inserted here. Some time ago I was commissioned to design and plant a trough 1ft x 4ft to go on a balcony in a large block of flats. I had only the dimensions of the space available, and was not informed that each flat had a similar balcony and that this one, on the ground floor, had above it a very large balcony; therefore, all the plants were deprived of top light and grew attenuated (straining outwards towards the light), and no rain reached the garden except when the wind blew it in that direction. So it should be emphasised that any obstruction above must be

17

taken into consideration when planning a balcony garden.

Roof gardens can be planted directly on to the surface if the latter is suitable and if there is adequate provision for any surplus moisture to drain away; most flat roofs have a channel to ensure this. If an ambitious design is planned with shallow beds contained by walling stone or standard concrete paving edges (these are available 36in long x 2in thick x 6in wide) which would give ample depth for drainage material and 4in to 5in of soil for the roots of the trees and plants. These blocks can be positioned and cemented on to the roof to make attractive shapes, or straight beds following the outline of the roof, but it is important that the weight should be spread evenly, preferably avoiding any excessive weight in the centre.

For anyone who has a flat roof, but cannot stoop to work with plants which are only 6in above ground-level, the alternative is to have a series of troughs on pedestals; in which case it is even more important that the weight is well away from the centre of the roof.

A combination of both these schemes was carried out on a

Fig 2

18

large flat roof of a gracious old house in London which transformed a dull area into a garden. The rectangular roof had a parapet about 36in high topped by square trellis for seclusion. There was a miniature trough garden on a pedestal either side of the French windows, and several of the same type positioned at irregular intervals on the opposite side. These were interspersed with long narrow troughs of varying heights, positioned to follow the shape of the roof, and planted with conifers and alpines on a slightly larger scale than those in the gardens on pedestals, so that from the ground-level they showed up more clearly (fig 2).

The area was spacious enough to have twelve of these gardens at ground-level (varying in height from 8in to 18in and in length from 30in to 40in) and still leave room in the centre for several chairs and a small table. The owner and guests could enjoy the impression of a fairly large town garden, with a very wide range of trees and plants flowering at different times of the year. Even on dull days, when viewed through the French windows from the dining-room, these gardens

Fig 3

19

were a source of great pride and pleasure to the owner.

A cavity wall built wide enough to have a good selection of trees and plants can be a most fascinating project. One such wall garden (fig 3), planted with different varieties of conifers, some compact cushion plants in between, and trailing plants tumbling over both the back and front walls, was made by an exceptionally generous gardener. She not only enjoyed the garden herself, but gave passers-by a rare and unexpected treat. This particular wall had a planting space of 12in and was very long, but the same scheme could be carried out on a more modest scale.

Another type of cavity wall can be constructed with varying levels; this is especially effective on a sloping site. Plate 3 shows one on three levels, but this idea leaves scope for a very wide range of designs to suit individual positions or sites, either on the flat or where an irregular surface presents a challenge.

2

CONTAINERS AND PEDESTALS

The scope and variety of containers is wide, ranging from a seed pan to a window-box or an old stone sink on a pedestal. The latter are excellent, as the mellow stone makes a perfect setting for the conifers and alpines, but unfortunately they are becoming scarce and consequently more expensive. Also, they have the disadvantage of being extremely heavy, generally needing two – sometimes four – strong men to lift one. Another drawback is that they usually have very thick walls (as much as 3in to 4in) which reduces the planting area.

A good substitute can be made of concrete and, if they are reinforced with wire or wire mesh, the walls need not be more than 1in thick. This not only makes them lighter to lift, but also allows more planting space than there is in a stone trough of the same outside dimensions. If the cement is mixed with very coarse sand, the concrete has an open texture which is porous and advantageous to the plants; also, when weathered, the concrete usually acquires a pleasing surface covered with mosses and lichens. We have some which are now very old and so mellowed that they are sometimes mistaken for genuine stone.

Concrete troughs can be made with very simple moulds of any size from 12in x 9in, up to 4ft or even more; but the inside depth need not be more than 3in. A very ambitious garden was made in a cast concrete trough 6ft x 3ft with well-designed supports of the same concrete mixture, so that when put together it was one complete unit in a rather spacious setting (fig 4).

Glazed sinks can be used if it is impossible to obtain a

21

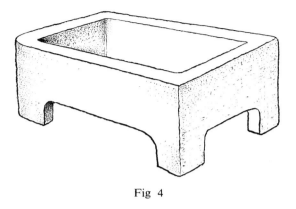

Fig 4

stone or concrete container. I have seen some trees and plants, lovingly tended by their owner, flourishing in glaring white glazed sinks and could not help thinking how much better they would have looked in a more harmonious setting. Glazed sinks – either white or a hideous yellow – are easily obtainable, and with a little trouble and moderate expenditure they can be made to look like stone by applying cement, as a paste, on top of a coat of bonding material (obtainable from most builders' merchants), as cement will not adhere to a glazed surface without the latter. First it is necessary to clean the sink thoroughly to ensure that there is no grease left on the surface, then apply the bonding material with a brush. Next, with a stippling movement, cover the area with the cement paste to give an effect of worn stone. Two, or even three, coats may be necessary to achieve the desired effect; an old short brush is the best for this process.

Containers of glass fibre are available; they are usually reproductions of lead or stone antiques, of good design, but seldom less than 8in to 12in deep, and so are not really suitable for a miniature garden. This excessive depth is out of proportion with the scale of the trees and plants and one is apt to see more of the container at first glance, than the actual garden. At the time of writing it is possible to have glass-fibre containers made to order, and these should be of simple lines and the same depth as advised for those made of concrete. These containers are rather expensive, but not more so than old stone sinks and they have two great advantages over the latter (a) they can be made of very thin section and yet are exceptionally strong, whereas old stone ones sometimes crack and (b) they are extremely light in weight and so are easily portable, which makes them well worth the extra cost. Glass fibre is obtainable in various gentle neutral colours which make a pleasant frame for the trees and plants.

The containers imported from Japan, especially for bonsai trees, are usually of very good design, shallow for their size, and of porous pottery glazed on the outside only, with drainage holes. These are ideal for small miniature gardens or for individual trees, but they are only obtainable from specialist importers.

For many years it was considered that porous clay pots and containers were essential for the well-being of trees and plants. My personal preference is for these stone or concrete troughs, but it must be admitted that trees and plants will flourish in plastic containers provided there is adequate drainage. Previously, I have been averse to using plastic because it was usually produced in such crude colours – harsh red, yellow, blue and green – the latter an insult to any growing plant. Fortunately, there are now some plastic trays in soft pleasing colours – grey, bisque and an unobtrusive olive green – and these do not clash with the delicate colours of the alpine plants. The trays have drainage holes so that the gardens are never waterlogged, and possibly the fact that these trays are easily cleaned and freed from lurking pests and fungi compensates for the lack of porosity in the sides.

One garden, planted in a dark grey plastic trough stayed out in the open all the time and, because there were several fair-sized drainage holes and adequate drainage material, it came through a period of excessive, almost tropical rain without any ill-effects. These plastic trays are very light, so that the garden is easily portable and suitable for indoor culture.

Asbestos cement containers are mass-produced in many different shapes and sizes, but as with the glass fibre ones most of them are far too deep and unsuitable for miniature gardens; they are usually planted with tulips, other bulbs and bedding plants. However, there is one size, 20in x 12in, which is only 2in deep and makes a splendid container for a small garden, as the depth is in proportion with the trees and plants. These particular containers are whitish in colour and quite inexpensive. Usually they do not have drainage holes, which are essential as this material is not really porous. One or two holes can easily be made with a suitable drill.

I have frequently been told about – and even been asked to judge – the entries in a competition for 'A Garden in a Soup Plate'. To me this idea is quite horrifying. The results are bits of plants with no roots, sometimes with pieces of mirror supposed to look like water; or if there are any plants with roots there is obviously no room for them. Moreover, as there is no drainage hole in a soup plate even small rooted plants can hardly be expected to survive after the competition.

A landscape in a raised bed gives more scope and a much wider range of trees and plants than is possible in a trough. If there is a suitable space in the garden to carry out this scheme the size and height will be governed by the space and materials available, as well as the time to do the actual preliminary work, but once this is done it will be very rewarding. The enclosure can be built of walling stone or old mellow bricks. If this is done in stages with gaps at irregular intervals, then some plants can be put in as the building of the wall progresses. The bricks or slabs should not be cemented, but if they have a firm foundation they can then be placed with each course slightly behind the one below, so that when the wall is finished there is a slight but definite slope backwards, ensuring that both light and water will reach the plants in the wall.

This type of planted wall is a matter of personal taste, but if the brick work is vertical, with no spaces for plants, it will then be simply an extension of a trough on a much larger scale. The shape of the bed could be a simple rectangle, or any decorative shape to suit the space available, or incorporate variations in different levels.

Pedestals can be made of mellow bricks or cement castings. Rick posts, or old chimney-pots, are decorative and usually a good height to support a trough garden. The square chimney-pots, with raised panels, and some of the very old round ones might almost have been designed for this purpose, as illustrated in plates 1 and 5. These and rick posts can sometimes be found in a demolition company's yard, or new ones can be purchased from a builder's merchant; it would be as well to avoid those of terracotta and aim at the biscuit-coloured ones which will eventually mellow to harmonise with old stone.

Searching in antique shops, or where old mansions are being demolished, will sometimes be rewarded by finding the graceful columns – balusters – of stone composition, cast in moulds, used in a series for parapets, balustrades, railings or bridges. They are generally single columns, but occasionally the more elaborate ones – as shown on the jacket – can be obtained

The simplest and cheapest supports for a large garden can be made of two columns of hollow concrete blocks, which are mass-produced and obtainable from most builders' merchants.

For the disabled gardener a special structure is essential. It must be sturdy and secure. It can be either made of two columns of brick or a special metal stand to support the garden, as described and illustrated in chapter 6.

3
DESIGN

A miniature garden can vary considerably and the design is, of course, a matter of personal taste, but as the whole layout can be seen in its entirety it is advisable for it to be planned to be interesting throughout the year. There is a very wide range of plants, some coming into flower in January or even December and others following on until the summer. The miniature roses, which commence to flower in the spring usually continue until late in the year. A few alpines flower through the summer and autumn and, if possible, some of these should be included; but it is also desirable to have some plants chosen for the colour and form of their foliage which will be decorative when no plants are in bloom. However small the garden there should be at least one conifer, as even in the depths of winter these are colourful and shapely.

There are endless possibilities, but whatever the scheme it is important to consider the value of space and proportion and to allow room for the plants to grow. Only the neatest and most compact plants, such as the Kabschia saxifraga, drabas and the smaller varieties of dianthus should be grown in association with the very slow-growing conifers, so that as the plants increase in area they are still in proportion with the trees and shrubs. Beginners, full of enthusiasm for the beauty of the trees, have a tendency to plant too many, too close together, for the size of the container; this sometimes has a detrimental effect on the conifers if the branches overlap, which causes them to grow one-sided and the congested foliage to turn brown. To avoid this it is advisable to allow sufficient space for them to grow without overcrowding and so display their handsome architectural structure.

Another choice which is to be considered before deciding on the design, is between a quick and mature effect, using trees and plants which, although classed as miniature, might outgrow the trough within a few years, and the really slow-growing alpines and conifers. Some people might prefer to furnish the garden with very young specimens of the latter type and so have the pleasure, spread over many years, of watching them grow, as they can be left in the garden indefinitely, but with the former types the garden might have to be replanted after a few years.

Whatever the design of garden it is important to keep the whole plan to scale. The trees and plants should be chosen to give balance and proportion in relation to one another as well as the container. The simplest type is a group of trees and plants – without any rocks or ornamental features – selected to give colour and variation at different times of the year. Another type of simple design is a garden without rocks, but just a winding path leading to an irregular-shaped pool with minute aquatics. A pendulous tree overhanging the water is most effective with marginal plants such as *Iris lacustris*, a miniature Forget-me-not (*Myosotis rupicola*), a very small rush (*Acorus gramineus* 'Pusillus') and some of the smallest ferns. The other trees, preferably those which are asymmetrical in habit, and plants filling the rest of the garden could include a miniature willow and miniature varieties of scillas, primulas and violets with other plants which look natural in association with each other and the water.

Pools of any size or shape can be made of glass fibre or other material which can be fabricated and will hold water, but not be affected by frost. A depth of not less than 2in must be allowed for the small aquatics. If the pool is large enough to have an island, this can be achieved by using a small clay pot – not plastic – disguised with a coat of cement and a few tiny pieces of rock affixed to the top. The acorus thrives as an aquatic, as well as a water-side plant; for a very small pool a rock which has moss already growing on it will generally flourish in water.

The rock garden in miniature is most popular, but it does need careful planning to obtain a really natural effect. Many would-be owners of a full-scale rock garden are thwarted by the cost of the rock and its transport, but the miniature gardener can select a few decorative weather-worn pieces of varying sizes for a moderate cost. They should be selected for their shapes, preferably with clefts and of a mellowed colour, which will make a good setting for the plants. The rocks and the trees should be positioned to look right before any of the plants are put in. It is difficult to move the rocks once the smaller plants are established. Trees of irregular and spreading habit, which will give a windswept effect, are the most suitable and they should be placed where they can be seen in profile, not in a valley, and even more important, not on the top of a hill. I have seen a slender symmetrical *Juniperus communis* 'Compressa' perched on the highest point of a garden where it looked quite incongruous; also in such a position there is the probability of the soil being washed away from the base of the trunk in heavy rain, thereby exposing the roots.

The trough should be prepared, as outlined in chapter 4, with enough soil to build up hills and valleys and the rocks sunk well into this – not at odd angles to each other in a haphazard fashion, but in such a way that they could give an impression that there was once a large block which has split naturally and the pieces moved apart by the plants which were growing in the cracks. This effect is enhanced if the stone has definite fissures or ridges all going in the same direction. If it is tufa rock then there are few ridges, but generally the shapes of the pieces will indicate how they should be placed in relation to one another. Tufa is very light and so porous that plants will grow into it, especially self-sown seedlings. When it is newly excavated it is usually almost white, and looks unnatural, but it will soon mellow and acquire a patina of soft brownish-green, more in keeping with the plants. The rocks should be well-submerged, not only to ensure that they remain securely in position, but because the submerged portion provides a cool root run, which is valuable for the welfare of the plants. Some larger pieces should stand well above the others and the spaces between them should be filled in to give an undulating effect, which is more natural for this type of garden.

Cushion plants, such as the Kabschia saxifraga, drabas and dianthus, are most effective when planted in the valleys close to the rocks and those of winding habit, like campanulas will trail in and out between the rocks, whilst others, like frankenia, pimelia and some of the smaller helianthemums, planted at the sides will cascade over the edges. Most old stone troughs have fairly thick walls and an irregular outer surface; with these the trailing plants are an embellishment, but with the type of container which is new with straight walls, the over-hanging plants are essential to conceal the hard lines.

A more ambitious rock garden can have the delightful addition of a waterfall leading to a rocky pool. To carry out this plan the garden must be spacious enough to have high rock work towards the back to conceal the pump and mechanism and to allow for small rocks to be built up in tiers, so that the water can trickle down and then be pumped up again when necessary. This is most effective if the highest point of the rock work is towards one end, so that the pool is not exactly central.

Formal gardens have a very strong appeal for those who have a flair for detailed construction on a miniature scale. An eminent gardener who generously praised some of my rock gardens was most disparaging about my formal designs, saying emphatically that they were not natural; but I ventured to point out to him that a full-scale formal garden was not natural and that, if neglected, would soon become a wilderness. However, many people find planning and planting formal gardens quite enthralling. For anyone who really enjoys designing, such a garden provides endless scope and pleasure, but this type of garden does need restraint as well as creative ability. It is so easy to make an elaborate plan and overwhelm the trees and plants with too many ornaments, or even paths. Whatever features are chosen it is essential that they should be in proportion with the garden as a whole. It is also important that the design should be to scale and in keeping with the container. The simple plan is usually the most successful and the easiest to maintain in good order. Any bird bath, sundial or statuette should be not only in proportion, but preferably a scale model of a classical design, such as would be found in a full-scale formal garden. It is better to alter the design rather than to use something which is quite incongruous, such as the whimsical 'gnomes' which, unfortunately, are seen too often. An alternative central feature can be a pool with miniature aquatics, of circular, semi-circular, square, rectangular or a special shape, as shown in fig 5. The paths surrounding the pool, or dividing the flower beds, can represent crazy paving or flagstones, but the two styles should not be mixed in one garden.

It would be helpful to make a rough sketch of your ideas before starting work on the garden; perhaps an easier way would be to cut out the shape of the proposed pool and paths in fairly stiff paper and then set them out in the container to make sure that the proportions are satisfactory. With this method any alterations can easily be carried out before it is too late.

Trees of symmetrical shape – *Juniperus communis* 'Compressa' or *Chamaecyparis thyoides* 'Andelyensis Nana' – are the most suitable for this type of garden; they can be planted in pairs and in such positions that they complement the design and are evenly balanced. Groups of plants such as erinus, the smaller varieties of dianthus and primulas, the pretty little annual Violet Cress (*Ionopsideum acaule*) and centauriums, and any other small plants which can be kept within bounds may be used to fill the flower beds.

To the rose-grower a fascinating development of the formal design is a rose garden in miniature. This can be set out with a number of small beds, divided by paths, each planted with a different variety of rose. It could be a circular design with the paths radiating from a central ornament, or with rectangular beds. If the container is more square than rectangular, then probably square beds would be in keeping. Anyone planning this type of garden and wishing to obtain a suitable model of a classical statue would need to search antique shops. I have collected bottle tops, seals and miniature figurines beautifully made of silver, which when weathered looks like lead and is most suitable for a garden ornament.

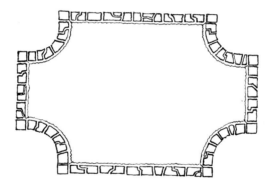

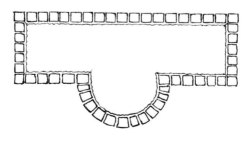

Fig 5

For anyone skilled in model work an attractive feature to make for a formal garden is a trellis, either made of wire, painted to represent wrought iron, or if made of wood this must be well seasoned and fastened together with waterproof glue. Whichever material is used, the structure must be securely fixed to the wall of the container so that it stands erect and supports the plants which are to be trained against it.

This type of garden requires deft fingers, and patience. It should not be undertaken by anyone without these two attributes, or equally important, the time to look after the plants: for they will need pruning and tying back to the trellis when necessary and this also applies to training over the arch. The bush roses must be discreetly pruned to keep them in proportion with the size of the beds and with each other. This is in addition to the usual care which roses require, cutting off dead blooms, checking for insect pests and applying a suitable insecticide if necessary. In fact, whether it is a rose garden or a formal garden with miniature flowerbeds described previously, it must be emphasised that this type of garden does need more care and attention than the rock garden in order to keep the symmetrical balanced effect.

A formal design does suggest a lawn, but as far as I know there is no true miniature grass. Several people have told me that they have used fine grass and clipped it with scissors to

Plate 1
Old stone sink, 63in x 27in x 6in; supported on three decorative chimney columns with *Chamaecyparis thyoides* 'Andelyensis', two *Juniperus communis* 'Compressa', one very old *Chamaecyparis obtusa* 'Nana Kosteri', with *Sempervivum arachnoideum* growing in a deep crevice in a large tufa rock, Kabschia saxifraga in variety, *Campanula cochlearifolia, Erinus alpinus, Potentilla eriocarpa,* and other alpines. *Dianthus myrtinervis, Paronychia serpyllifolia* and *Pimelia coarctata* overhanging the front. June

Plate 2
Garden in a concrete trough, 48in x 36in x 4in, with a central pool and arch at each end. Placed in front of a window, seen a year after planting, with some of the miniature daffodils in flower. See plate 8

34

keep it close to the ground. They did not realise that grass roots take up a lot of goodness from the soil and that, once established, it is difficult to prevent it from invading the rest of the garden, so I suggest that this should be avoided. If it is desirable to introduce the effect of a miniature lawn into the design, there are two other plants which are more suitable. The first is *Arenaria balearica* which grows flat on the ground with minute bright-green leaves; it does spread fairly quickly, but as the roots are very fine and near the surface it is easily controlled by cutting through any excess with

Plate 3 top left
Garden on three levels, 14ft long, 15in wide, constructed to coincide with three broad steps. This garden could be viewed and enjoyed from the house as well as on the lawn below. The top garden has a semi-circular pool with aquatics and is flanked on either side by a *Juniperus communis* 'Compressa'; groups of miniature roses surround the pool and there is a *Chamaecyparis obtusa* 'Nana' at each end. The second tier has an *Acer palmatum* 'Dissectum Atropurpureum' and the green form at the other end, each surrounded with bolder alpines. The lowest tiers were planted with one larger conifer in each section with some miniature daffodils and trailing alpines to overhang the sides

Plate 4 top right
Concrete trough, 20in x 12in on cast pedestal, with *Abies lasiocarpa* 'Compacta', *Rosa* Peon, *Mimulus primuloides, Campanula pulla, Rhodohypoxis baurii, Erinus alpinus* and *Asperula suberosa.* June

Plate 5 bottom left
Concrete trough, 36in x 24in x 4in on a square chimney pedestal, with *Juniperus communis* 'Compressa', *Picea mariana* 'Nana', *Cassiope mertensiana, Rosa* Cinderella, *R.* Elf and *R.* Roulettii, *Campanula arvatica, Androsace sempervivoides, Potentilla eriocarpa, Centaurium portense, Scilla verna,* various saxifraga and *Artemisia brachyphylla* and *Asperula gussoni* and *Pimelia coarctata* in the front. May

Plate 6 bottom right
Sandstone sink, 30in x 20in x 6in on a chimney pedestal with *Picea abies* 'Nidiformis', *Erinus alpinus, Campanula* x Norman Grove, *Helianthemum oblongatum, Raoulia australis* – the silver foliage in striking contrast to the vivid red of *Sempervivum arenarium* and *Pimelia coarctata.* June

35

a pair of sharp scissors and gently pulling away what is not required. In April/May it bears myriads of tiny white flowers on 1in hair-like stems. These are pretty, but if it is to represent a miniature lawn, the height of the stems destroy the illusion and they can be cut back close to the foliage.

For a sunny position *Raoulia lutescens* is the best 'lawn' plant; it is so minute – more like a film of grey-green covering the earth – and much more slow-growing than the former. This raoulia requires patience to achieve the right effect, as it is usually pot-grown and several plants may be required to cover the desired area. As the foliage is quite microscopic, it is necessary that each plant should be level with its neighbour to obtain the continuous effect. Some fine sand sprinkled on any spaces between the plants will help new growth to cover these and so make a complete carpet.

Children's gardens should be simple in design to encourage a real interest in the trees and plants, which might be diverted by too many ornaments. If the garden is furnished with a selection of trees and plants which are reasonably hardy and not difficult to maintain it will need just enough care to sustain their interest to watch it grow and develop.

Some children are fascinated by the miniature trees and plants; they really enjoy planning, planting and looking after a garden of their own. If they are observant this will encourage them to notice the seasonal changes of the plants, and to study the wondrous design of the different species. The knowledge that some of these alpine plants originated in many different parts of the world stimulates their imagination. In each case where I have designed and planted a garden especially for a school or for disabled children, we have sent with it a key drawing, and a list of the plants, giving their botanical names and the country of origin. One teacher told me, with enthusiasm, that he would use such a plan in a geography lesson.

If the garden is for one child only an additional attraction is, if possible, to incorporate a tree of approximately the same age as the child; this seldom fails to delight the young owner, even if the tree does eventually outgrow the garden. I was once shown a tree with such a history, which had been the proud possession of a young man for over fifteen years, as his father had given it to him when he was a small boy.

For a group of children at home, in a school or hospital, the garden should be large enough for several of them to gather round it. If the design incorporates a path leading to a model cottage or a pool, perhaps with a bridge, then these should be part of the design and in proportion for the size of the garden, not added in a haphazard fashion after planting. This might detract from the beauty of the trees and plants. Sometime ago I made a garden for a school for children, who had recently been taken to see a real windmill, which they found enthralling, so I introduced a path leading to a working model of a windmill (plate 13); the landscape was designed as a setting for this one model only.

Water is always an attraction and a pond with some minute aquatics adds to the interest for the children. In another school a group of children were planning a little landscape for themselves and they made some quite charming models – a cottage and a path leading to a pool – in their pottery class (plate 12).

I have stressed the importance of simplicity of design – models of a cottage, windmill or path leading to a bridge over a pool should be used with discretion – so that the trees and plants are not overwhelmed by too many distractions. This is, unfortunately, too often seen in a rash of Japanese houses, bridges and little figures and, worst of all, a piece of mirror to represent water, the plants frequently a mixture of cacti, ivies and other plants which not only require different conditions, but are not true miniatures and give an impression that such gardens are only toys. For the true miniature garden the trees and plants should be the dominant part of the landscape and a real pool – any small bowl which will hold water – is so much more effective than a piece of mirror and can have some minute aquatics.

37

4

PREPARING AND PLANTING
THE GARDEN

The best time to plant a new garden is the early autumn, as this allows the plants to become established before the winter and so able to withstand any extremes of weather. With the autumn planting the owner will have the pleasure of seeing the early spring alpines coming into flower. One of the miniature daffodils (*Narcissus asturiensis*) usually blooms in January and February, followed by the enchanting spring saxifraga, the miniature willows and many others.

If it is not possible to leave the planting until the autumn, then the early spring will give the plants time to be established before the hot weather. At this time of the year it is advisable to select young pot plants, rather than those which are in full flower and might wilt after transplanting. In most commercial nurseries the trees and plants are pot grown so that they can be transplanted at any time of the year. Obviously it is undesirable to do this when there is danger of frost, or alternatively, in excessively hot weather.

Sometimes one might wish to plant a garden during the school holidays, or for a present on a special occasion, at a time of the year when conditions are not favourable; then the newly planted garden does need extra care. If there is a danger of frost, covering the garden with polythene at night should protect it until this danger has passed. If the garden is to be planted during very hot weather, it should be watered generously both morning and evening and, if it is in full sun, a temporary shade put over it until it is well-established and the plants are not flagging. Some people do not understand that trees and plants which have been moved in extremes of weather, do need this extra care.

If the plants are not pot grown – perhaps gifts from friends who have a surplus, or conifers from the open ground – then it would be advisable to delay the planting until the autumn, when the conifers are dormant, because it is not possible to lift these without disturbing the roots, as it is with a pot-grown specimen.

Whatever size the garden, the procedure is much the same. Good drainage is essential, for these trees and plants will not tolerate being waterlogged. If the garden is fairly large and is to be planted in its permanent position, it is advisable to check the level of the base inside by pouring some water in to ensure that it has a clear run through. This is especially important with old stone sinks, which are sometimes worn at one end, or concave in the middle, where any surplus water might remain. If the hollow is at one end, a small wedge beneath the sink should compensate for this without the tilt being apparent,

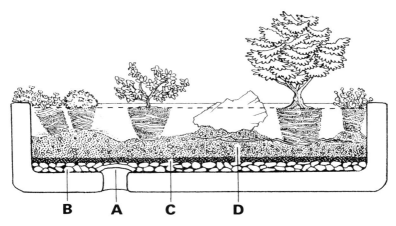

Fig 6   Section through trough showing planting materials
    A   Drainage hole covered with convex piece of flower-pot
    B   Drainage layer of pebbles
    C   Peat
    D   Potting compost

but if the hollow is very deep, or in the middle, then extra drainage can be used to fill this in.

First, the drainage hole should be covered with a large convex piece of broken flower-pot, to prevent the drainage material and soil seeping through, but to allow any excess water to do so. Some writers advise perforated zinc to cover the drainage hole, but I have found that plants' roots become entangled in this and cannot be released without damage; the piece of flower-pot, positioned so that the water can run under the curve, is safer. Next, the base should be covered with a layer of drainage material, which can be either pebbles or small pieces of broken flower-pot; if the latter, it is advisable to wash the pots before smashing them to be sure that there is no risk of introducing any pests or fungi into the garden. Over the drainage material add a layer of peat, which will absorb some of the moisture and also form a 'blanket' to prevent the compost from trickling down and clogging the drainage material, so defeating its sole object which is to allow excess moisture to drain away (fig 6).

For a general collection of conifers and alpines, John Innes Potting Compost No 2 is the most suitable. Some of this can be spread over the top of the peat, bringing it to about half-way, or two-thirds of the inside depth, then water thoroughly and allow time for the peat to absorb the moisture – which will cause it to swell – and the compost to settle, so eliminating any air-pockets.

If it is to be a rock garden, then the next stage is for the rocks to be positioned so that they are partially buried when the extra compost is added. Then the trees can be placed in relation to the rocks. Should they be pot bound, the roots very much tangled, and the earth between them seems exhausted, it is advisable to shake out gently all the old earth and dis-entangle the roots. (If this is not done they might remain in the tight ball and not take up any nutrient or make new growth.) They can then be spread across the bed of compost prepared for them and lightly covered (fig 7).

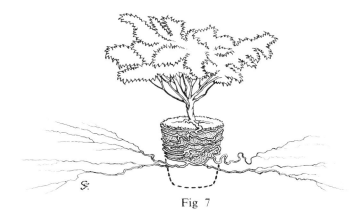

Fig 7

Next, put in any shrubs or roses, then the 'cushion' plants to nestle between the rocks. The plants such as campanulas and hypsella will wind their way hither and thither and fill in the spaces. Lastly, put in the trailing plants which have been selected to overhang the sides of the trough. The base of the tree-trunk and the 'collar' of the plants should be carefully positioned for height in relation to the top of the container. If they are too high then the surrounding soil might be washed away in heavy rain, exposing the roots; if too low the submerged portion might become muddied and weakened, causing rot, so spoiling their appearance. Also, if the trailing plants are too low they could not produce the desired effect, cascading over the sides.

When they are all satisfactorily positioned and soil added to bring it to the correct level – just below the top of the trough – it is desirable to firm down around each tree and plant and, if necessary, add a little more of the compost to keep the level as required. Then the whole area can be covered with a top dressing of chippings. These chippings serve a double purpose; they conserve the moisture, preventing the soil from drying out too quickly in hot weather, and also protect the low growing plants from being splashed with mud

41

in heavy rain. Finally, brush off any soil which may have been spilled on the foliage and water gently, but thoroughly, preferably using a can with a fine rose.

The method of preparing for planting a formal garden – or one with paths and a pool or other ornament – is quite different, for it is important that these features should be positioned and securely affixed to the base of the container before any drainage material is put in. It would be difficult to bring these to the desired height and level, except on a reasonably flat surface. A pool might warp or crack if it rested on uneven drainage material, so it must be supported carefully. If it is for a large garden then it should be about 1in less in depth than the inside of the container; it can rest on a bed of about $\frac{1}{2}$in sieved peat or sand, then the top of the pool will be about a $\frac{1}{2}$in below the top of the trough so that the plants surrounding the pool can rise just a little above its rim.

If the paths are part of an elaborate design they are best made seperately and, whatever the width, they should not be less than 1in in depth or they may crack in frosty weather. They can be supported at intervals by inverted flower-pots, preferably cemented to the base. If they are positioned and resting on the soil without any permanent supports they will probably sink if the soil should shrink in hot dry weather. A length of wood with a straight edge resting across the top of the trough will indicate if the levels of the pool and paths are correct or need any adjustment before the next stage. Also, any trellis, archway or miniature statue should be fixed to the trough at these preliminary stages. When this preparatory work is satisfactorily concluded the intervening spaces at the base of the trough can now be covered with drainage material, then a layer of peat, and on this a layer of compost, watered thoroughly and left to settle before the actual planting is commenced, which can be carried out as outlined earlier in this chapter.

5

CARE OF THE GARDEN

Looking after a trough garden is real gardening and is as important – perhaps even more so – than the routine work carried out in a full-scale garden; because, if neglected, a miniature garden might be more difficult to restore to its original condition. If the work outlined in the following pages is carried out regularly, the garden should flourish and never reach the neglected stage. If possible daily attention will enable the owner to observe the growth and development of the trees and plants.

Watering is the most important requirement, for it must be emphasised that in a trough garden, the roots of the trees and plants cannot go down in search of moisture – during a dry period – as they can do in the open ground. Therefore, it is essential that a garden with such limitations should never be allowed to dry out. Most of the alpines will revive after a good soaking, but it is much more serious for the conifers, as once they have suffered for any length of time from lack of moisture they deteriorate rapidly and might never recover.

One of the questions most frequently put to me is 'How often should I water the garden?' It is impossible to answer this satisfactorily. There are so many factors to consider: the time of the year, the condition of the plants – if they are growing and flowering or resting – the size and depth of the garden and, of course, if there has been much or little rain. The only safe guide is that it is better to over-water than risk the plants becoming too dry, because if the garden has been properly prepared with adequate drainage and a porous soil, any excess water will soon seep away.

If, due to the absence or illness of the owner, the garden has been neglected and the soil become too dry it will appear to have shrunk, because as the moisture evaporates the particles which make up the compost come closer together, usually leaving cracks and, even worse, gaps between the walls of the trough and the compost. Then, when the garden is watered much is wasted, as it runs through these spaces and is of very little benefit to the garden. If this condition should arise, the best method of preventing this waste and danger to the plants – exposing the roots – is to prick gently over the surface to allow a little air to enter and also to push the compost against the walls of the trough before watering, after which the compost will usually swell out to its previous condition. But it may be necessary to add some to compensate for the shrinkage.

In hot weather it is wiser to water in the early morning or evening, as hot sun through a drop of water on the foliage acts as a burning glass, causing scorch. In excessively hot weather the plants in a small garden may flag during the day, before it is safe to water. To prevent this happening, damping down around the garden to cool the air, and so reduce evaporation from the leaves, will help the plants to withstand the heat until it is safe to water. If the timing should be difficult then it is possible to pour water gently *between* the plants to ensure that the roots get the benefit, but the foliage is not damped in full sun and subjected to the danger of scorch.

In winter, if there should be a prolonged dry spell when the buds are forming on the early spring flowering alpines, it may be necessary to water the garden; but of course it is only safe to do so on a bright sunny day, about midday, but never if there is danger of frost. Sometimes, after a hard frost, the earth rises up in stiff ridges near the base of the trees and plants, exposing the roots, also leaving a gap between these and the walls of the container. If this condition should arise it requires most careful attention, but *not* until the earth has thawed, because of the danger of breaking the roots which

Fig 8   Selection of useful tools

would be frozen in the solid earth. After the thaw it is important to prick gently over the earth and press it back to its normal condition, if necessary adding a little to compensate for wastage.

When working with these small plants it is desirable to have a few special tools. The most useful are:

(a)   A watering-can with a very fine rose to give a steady and gentle flow. Unfortunately, the tiny holes tend to become blocked with minute particles of dust, but the rose is usually detachable and can be cleaned by submerging it in a bowl of warm water.

(b)   A spray, or syringe, for damping the foliage and for use with insecticides.

(c)   A small fern trowel.

(d)   A small fork – the type which is usually sold with the trowel is too big and clumsy for alpines. I have found an old bone-handled fish fork the perfect tool, especially suitable for weeding.

45

(*e*) A pair of forceps for removing the smallest weeds in their early stages, especially from the 'cushion' plants where they are extremely difficult to eradicate once they start to grow. The forceps are also useful for removing any parts affected by mildew or botrytis.

(*f*) A small paint-brush for removing earth from low growing plants after first planting or replanting.

(*g*) A magnifying glass for identifying insect pests.

Plants which are usually classed as weeds in an ordinary garden may grow from seeds either blown in by the wind or were already in the soil when the garden was planted. Any seedlings which appear soon after this should be removed at once. Those which germinate later can be regarded with a little more tolerance until identified, as they may be seedlings of one of the plants already established.

Fig 9   *Oxalis repens*

To state quite definitely what is a weed is rather difficult, because it may truly be said that one man's weed is another man's treasure. Any plant which grows too rapidly and will encroach upon its neighbours, should be sternly regarded as a weed when considering a true miniature garden. There are many charming plants, such as the thymes, delightful in a large rock garden or in paving but which, if left to their own devices in a small sink garden, will soon envelop it.

Oxalis repens (fig 9), with its tiny yellow flowers and small clover-like leaves, charms the innocent to leave it; whereupon it proceeds to flower madly, catapulting its seeds with surprising velocity, and before the owner realises what is happening he or she has an oxalis garden. Its habit of twining its roots and stems amongst the foliage and roots of other plants make it difficult to eradicate.

Sagina procumbens (fig 10), usually known as pearlwort, starts life as a minute cluster of slender leaves looking rather like a group of microscopic green stars which were not there before. Unless you have been warned you may be tempted to look after them, but if you leave these little seedlings they will soon grow into clusters bearing tiny greenish-white flowers and, before you can say 'Chamaecyparis!' they will shed thousands of seeds which will germinate with disastrous efficiency. All your close growing plants will have become

Fig 10   *Sagina procumbens*

infested to such an extent that a tight green mat of this pernicious weed can eventually smother the entire garden, so every minute piece must be carefully removed. This is where the forceps are invaluable as they will facilitate the removal of this weed without disturbing the roots of the choice alpines.

Cardamine hirsuta (fig 11), or 'Poppers', has white flowers and slender seed pods, which when ripe scatter their seeds far and wide. This plant, although as prolific as the others, is not so tiresome to remove as it comes up quite easily with one sharp pull.

Insect pests, if left unchecked, can do a great deal of damage to miniature trees, roses and alpines. Aphids, and Scale insects, are easily identified, but Red-spider mite, even more devastating is not so easily recognised; partly because it usually

Fig 11   *Cardamine hirsuta*

remains on the under surface of the leaves of the roses and alpines and in between the tiny leaves of the conifers, but mostly because it is so very minute. Although they are hardly visible to the naked eye the effect of their presence can be deduced by the mottled, yellowish patches of the foliage. If left uncontrolled, they can completely defoliate the plant. They are more prevalent in hot dry weather and frequent damping of the foliage will reduce the possibility of attack, but if there is an indication that they are attacking the plants, a piece of the foliage should be examined under a magnifying glass to identify them. It is easy to be misled, as they are not really spiders and only red at one stage of their life – more often they are green and sometimes one can only see the microscopic globular eggs. Red-spider mite should not be confused with a very beautiful coral-red velvety spider, known as red velvet mite, a friendly insect, which moves quickly on the soil, and is easily visible as it is larger than red-spider mite.

Scale insects sometimes attack conifers, and an indication of their presence is the rather dingy appearance of the foliage and patches of sooty mould which grows on the honeydew excreted by these insects. They look like minute mussels and remain stationary in clusters on the foliage and stems, extracting the sap from the tissues of the plants.

Soil pests – slugs, millepedes, wireworms and woodlice – sometimes attack plants in pots which are at ground-level, but they very seldom reach gardens on pedestals unless introduced with a pot plant. Woodlice are the most dangerous, as they are not obvious, but usually increase rapidly in a space under a rock and gather under prostrate plants.

The most common *friendly* insects are the lace-wing fly, the ladybird, all garden spiders and the centipede; the latter is unfortunately often mistaken for a millepede, but it is easily identified because it moves rapidly whereas the former usually coils up like a spiral spring.

Botrytis (grey mould) is a fungus which sometimes grows on decaying or damaged foliage, more so with plants under glass than in the open. Affected parts should be cut off – removed with care to prevent any spores scattering on other plants – and burned. Then the plant should be dusted with a fungicide.

Mildew may attack plants, especially roses, at any time of the year, but it is more prevalent when the plant is subjected to extremes of temperature, when a cold night follows a sunny day or the artificial heat of a living room drops to extreme cold. Mildew is a white mealy growth producing innumerable spores which can be carried in the air. It is most important to cut off all affected foliage and buds and burn them. A fungicide can then be applied, either in a liquid solution syringed on the plant, or a powder form dusted on the affected parts is preferable in cold weather.

There are numerous insecticides available and once the pest or fungus is identified the appropriate control measures can be used. Care should be taken not to exceed the dosage recommended by the makers, as too strong an application might be very harmful to the small plants.

Pruning of miniature roses will be found described in greater detail in chapter 9. Some of the other flowering shrubs may also need pruning and the best time is after flowering, but it

Plate 7 top
Formal garden in a concrete trough, 48in x 36in x 4in, with a central pool at the back of which is a model 'temple', flanked by a pair of *Juniperus communis* 'Compressa' (approximately twenty-five years old, they have been in this garden since 1956) with a row of *Rosa* Peon along the back. Each end of the pool the small rush, *Acorus gramineus* 'Pusillus' and between them a row of *Erinus alpinus* along each side of the pool. In front a semi-circle of *Rhodohypoxis baurii* edged with *Dianthus* Prince Charming. Behind each *Chamaecyparis obtusa* 'Nana' there are two rows of *Rosa* Elf and *R.* Cinderella. July

Plate 8 bottom
Close-up of the trough garden in plate 2. Roses are trained over the arches, with bush roses either side of the pool. The paths and the pool are edged with *Saxifraga aizoon* 'Baldensis'. *Chamaecyparis pisifera* 'Nana' at each corner at the back and *C. thyoides* 'Andelyensis Nana' at each corner in the front. Various alpines, to flower at different times of the year, in between the trees. June

might be desirable to remove any unhealthy branchlets – or coarse growth – to keep the bush compact and shapely at any time of the year. Regular pruning is seldom necessary for the slow growing shrubs, such as cassiope or jasminum, but some of the quicker growing species, like salix or syringa, usually need to be cut back to keep them shapely and in proportion with the other trees and plants.

It is unusual, but some of the slow-growing, evergreen conifers have been known to produce a branchlet which has reverted to coarse growth. Contrary to a popular fallacy that this only happens on grafted trees, it does occur on trees grown on their own roots. In each case the branchlet which is out of character should be removed. Some visitors to this Nursery seem convinced that the really old specimens of *Juniperus communis* 'Compressa' which we have treasured for many years, have been clipped to induce their elegant shape.

Plate 9 top
Old stone sink, 36in x 24in, with *Chamaecyparis obtusa* 'Filicoides' (the Fern spray cypress) and a collection of small hardy ferns; in the background *Viola hederacea* is flowering happily in September

Plate 10 middle
Concrete trough, 36in x 24in x 4in, constructed on two levels with a minute 'dry wall' supporting the rose bed in front of the trellis. Silver Grecian figurine, 3in high, beneath the arch, steps leading to pool edged with *Saxifraga aizoon* 'Baldensis', *Hydrocharis morsus-ranae* floating on the surface. Campanulas, dianthus and other small alpines in the lower level garden. In the foreground two good specimens of *Chamaecyparis obtusa* 'Nana' and *Raoulia lutescens* representing a lawn in the centre. June

Plate 11 bottom
Concrete trough, 36in x 18in, with a rectangular pool and a bed with a radius at each corner to support enough compost to provide marshy conditions for *Acorus gramineus* 'Pusillus'. *Chamaecyparis obtusa* 'Pygmaea' in the centre at the back, with young specimens of *Juniperus communis* 'Compressa' and a pair of *Chamaecyparis obtusa* 'Nana'. Rose bushes along the back and in the beds either side of the pond. In the foreground a group of *Primula scotica* and *Rhodohypoxis baurii*, with other small alpines around the conifers

whereas this can only be produced by nature, allowing the trees to grow slowly and naturally without any feeding. The pair in plate 7 have been in that trough – which is only 3in inside depth – for over twenty years and they were approximately five years old when planted and are now 26in high.

Lifting and dividing is routine work in large-scale gardening, but some people do not realise that this also applies to plants on a miniature scale if they should grow too vigorously. They seem surprised and sometimes almost resentful of the fact that a plant which is small in all its parts will eventually – if healthy – spread so that it might need to be controlled. A garden which is planted for immediate effect, with fairly quick-growing plants will require this attention sooner than one which contains the more slow-growing types. A plant which romps away in one garden might remain almost stationary in different conditions; in fact, what is almost a weed in one garden can be a 'miff' elsewhere. Also, sad to say it must be acknowledged that some plants are short-lived.

When a garden has reached the stage where some of the trailing plants, such as campanula, frankenia or paronychia may have spread too much and will be crowding the cushion plants, the time to lift and divide those which are encroaching upon their neighbours would be after flowering. The best part of the plant can be replaced, taking care to give the roots ample room, and the surplus potted up or planted out elsewhere. Some plants, such as erodium, have one main root and cannot be divided; so if they begin to grow too near their neighbours, it is a good plan to take a few cuttings before removing the old plant.

Fertilisers should be used sparingly on trough gardens. People who are accustomed to herbaceous borders or rose gardens think automatically of manuring their gardens at regular intervals, not realising that in their natural habitat many alpines grow in poor soil and only receive a top dressing of any decaying foliage which may be washed down upon them. My own experience of growing alpines and conifers in troughs has convinced me that too rich a soil or too much fertiliser encourages unnaturally luxuriant growth and a loss of the compact habit and possibly a loss of strength and sturdiness. If the garden has been planted in a good compost with adequate drainage – to eliminate the possibility of the soil becoming sour – it should be healthy for five or six years without any additional feeding. The two conifers referred to in the section on pruning had no fertilisers added; only an occasional top dressing of John Innes Compost No 2.

If it is obvious that some plants are not flourishing and the foliage is limp and a poor colour, it is advisable to inspect the plant carefully for insect pests, because if these are present it is useless to give the plant any form of fertiliser until they are dealt with. If any pests are seen, then the appropriate control measures should be taken without delay, but if the plant is free of pests it can then be assumed that it needs some form of fertiliser. It is inadvisable to use this too freely because, as mentioned previously, this may encourage very coarse growth and also if the plant is in poor condition, it is likely that the roots may not be able to take up the extra feed, which if not used could only throw the compost out of balance.

The poor colour of the foliage, especially with conifers, is sometimes an indication of a soil deficiency – usually magnesium – and this can be rectified by spraying the foliage with magnesium sulphate (Epsom salts), half a teaspoonful to a pint of water. With ample spraying some of the solution will seep into the soil and the plants may absorb this through the roots as well as the foliage. Even if you are in doubt as to the cause of the trouble, this treatment cannot do any harm and in most cases it is beneficial. If it does not produce results after, say, three applications at weekly intervals, then a small dose of fertiliser could be tried.

The easiest type of fertiliser to use on a small garden is one which is soluble, so that it can be mixed at the correct strength and watered evenly over the garden; but if the soil is already wet then the solution is diluted, or if too much were poured around one particular plant the result would be an excessive concentration. A powder form of fertiliser is a little more trouble, but it is much simpler to control the dosage. Although Tonks Rose Fertiliser is a special preparation for roses, I have found it beneficial for other plants. For small alpines, a saltspoonful spread around the base and gently forked in is generally sufficient.

6

GARDENS FOR THE ELDERLY
OR DISABLED

It is difficult for anyone who is fit and able to garden happily without fatigue – other than the healthy tiredness which follows a session of gardening – to understand the frustration of being deprived of the very great satisfaction that such work can bring. To elderly gardeners who can no longer stoop or kneel, the ground seems far away and they may feel that their gardening days are over. With a trough garden raised up to a convenient level they can recapture the pleasure of growing their own plants and seeing them come into bud and flower through the seasons.

As mentioned earlier, the charm and beauty of the miniature trees and plants can only be appreciated if they are near enough to be observed in detail. I was once told by the grand-daughter of a famous gardener how, when he was old and rather frail, she would push his wheelchair to the rock garden for him to see some of his favourite plants. It was a special ceremony for her to arrange pieces of mirror around the soldanellas, so that he could see the reflection of these enchanting little fringed bells from his chair. Her description was so vivid that one could almost share his pleasure. I think that this would have been so much greater if he could have had some of these plants raised up in a trough garden; then he would have seen these exquisite flowers on their graceful, pendulous stems in full detail, as well as some of his other favourites.

Some disabled people who have previously led active lives, with different interests and hobbies other than horticulture, have suddenly been deprived of these activities and, after a period of depression and emptiness, discovered a new world in this form of gardening. Others, who have been handicapped from childhood and never experienced the pleasure of gardening, have found the miniature trees and plants a revelation, a source of interest and satisfaction which cannot be compared with anything else.

One invalid who had been confined to her room for many years always had a profusion of florists' flowers and pot plants around her, but had never seen plants growing until a relative decided to have a miniature garden made for her to fit on the window-ledge. In this garden she could see the early bulbs emerging into flower in January and February and then the spring alpine plants, followed by the miniature roses coming into bloom, in their seasons. Her room was on the fourth floor and she was concerned that this window-ledge was too exposed, so she sent for a carpenter to fix a glass wind-break at each end of the window-ledge at right-angles to the window. This was very successful as it allowed the maximum of light and the plants flourished, bringing the owner a new and absorbing hobby.

From the many courageous people I have been privileged to meet in person, or by correspondence, I can realise the very great difference these gardens have made to those who otherwise would be unable to enjoy growing plants. Another invalid, who was so ill that she could not negotiate the stairs, had a room on the ground floor, with French windows opening out on to a terrace, turned into her bedroom. She had a long narrow miniature garden supported on two columns on this terrace where she could see the profile of the trees and the plants from her bed. On the days when she was well enough she could sit beside the garden in her wheelchair. Before she became so ill she was well known for her designs and line drawings so, as an artist, these engaging little plants brought her a new delight in studying their beauty. Later, her sister wrote to me that this garden had been a very great pleasure and solace to her to the end of her life.

Plate 12 top
Garden for a school for disabled children, 48in x 24in x 4in, with a weatherproof model cottage and path leading from this to a bridge over a pool, bordered by tiny ferns and rushes. The conifers are *Picea mariana* 'Nana', *Juniperus communis* 'Compressa', *Chamaecyparis obtusa* 'Nana Kosteri'. Roses in variety, saxifraga of different colours behind the path, *Primula scotica* and other small alpines in front of the path. May

Plate 13 bottom
A garden for children, 48in x 24in, with a path leading to a working model windmill. *Chamaecyparis obtusa* 'Nana', *C. thyoides* 'Andelyensis', *Cassiope tetragona*, roses in variety, *Centaurium portense*, *Primula scotica, Ionopsideum acaule, Rhodohypoxis baurii*, campanulas, dianthus and saxifrages in variety

59

The sign in the image reads:

MINIATURE GARDEN DESIGNED & MADE BY
MISS ANNE ASHBERRY. *AUTHOR OF GARDENS ON A HIGHER LEVEL*
IS A WISHING WELL GIFT TO
Danby House Residential Home *FOR*
the Handicapped. EXMOUTH.
& IT WILL BE ERECTED ON A PEDESTAL AT THE
HOME TO ENABLE WHEELCHAIR CASES TO ATTEND TO IT AND
THEREBY PROVIDE THEM WITH AN INTEREST IN GARDENING

Plate 14
Garden presented by Mr Porter to a home for disabled adults. The
two little girls seem absorbed in the miniature trees and plants.

60

A young boy wrote to me from a school for disabled children to ask for my help in planning a garden which he and a group of other handicapped children wished to make in a 4ft sink which had been given to them. The Headmistress had had it erected on a sturdy structure of angle iron, which allowed ample room for several children, in their wheelchairs, to work comfortably at the planting of the garden and its subsequent care. We sent them a suitable collection of trees and plants – each correctly labelled – together with a key drawing. The garden was duly planted and this project brought a new interest to the group 'of children who worked on it.

Some time later the boy who had initiated the scheme wrote to me reporting on the progress of the garden and asking my advice about the 'Mesembryanthemum' because it was 'bumping into some other plants' and also asking about using a fungicide on what they thought might be mildew. This indicated to me that their interest had not waned and that the children were not only conversant with the botanical names of the plants, but were really anxious to know if the plants should be cut back or divided and how to treat mildew. They were, in fact, becoming real gardeners. The letter was laboriously produced on a typewriter and in it he told me that they had made some minute hedgehogs in their pottery class and these were now in their garden and they had made a bird-bath which they were sending to me. This arrived and I do treasure it, because the little birds resting on the rim are beautifully coloured and the bird-bath itself had been made with loving care.

For the elderly who cannot stand for long – and even more so for the disabled – the trough garden should be at a height which enables the gardener to work comfortably seated, without straining or stooping. For the wheel-chair gardener the position and height of the garden requires careful consideration to suit individual needs. Both the height and the length of the trough, as well as the distance between the supports, should be planned to allow the wheel-chair to be manoeuvred comfortably as though the gardener was seated at a table. The supports of two columns of brick or concrete, but preferably a metal frame as shown in fig 12, must be sturdily built and stand on a level site so that there is no danger of the garden tilting and falling.

If the position is against a wall, then this will govern the width of the garden to ensure that the plants at the back can be within easy reach; but if the garden can be approached both from the back and the front then the width could be approximately doubled. Some standard containers are from 6in to 8in deep, but if the base is above the gardener's knees this brings the planting surface too high for comfortable working. The distance between the knees and the top of the container should be planned – as near as possible – so that

Fig 12

the gardener can work with hands outstretched and the fore-arms horizontal. Working with the hands above elbow-level for any length of time is tiring even for an able-bodied person, but would be quite exhausting for anyone who is handicapped. The trough need not be more than 4in deep; this brings the working surface to a comfortable level and also reduces the weight of soil which would be very heavy in a deeper container. As shown in most of the illustrations dwarf conifers and alpines will flourish in a shallow container provided they are never allowed to become too dry.

In most prefabricated troughs the drainage holes are central, but as this may allow any excess moisture to seep through onto the gardener's knees it is important to avoid this by having the drainage holes at the extreme corners. If the container is cast in concrete or glass fibre, it is possible to make an improvement by having little channels formed in the base to cross diagonally from corner hole to corner hole.

Some years ago a Mr Porter wrote to me about miniature plants and sent me photographs and press cuttings about his collection of trough gardens, which were displayed in his front garden in Exmouth. Amidst the trough gardens he had a large wishing-well, and he found that people passing on their way to the sea-front would drop pennies in the well. He put up a notice specifying certain charities which would benefit from the proceeds. The first target was to purchase a caravan for some handicapped people to have a seaside holiday. Then he raised enough money to add two more caravans to local sites and later sufficient for more caravans for different holiday places throughout the country. I was able to send him the plants he wished to have to add to his collection of miniature gardens, which became more and more widely known and the means of raising vast sums for various charities. Mr Porter was later awarded the MBE for his splendid services to many causes.

Knowing my interest in his work, he asked me to design and plant a trough garden for him to present to a Home for disabled adults which was to be opened in his district within a few months. In view of the magnificent results he had obtained from his wishing well, I suggested that a model well should be the decorative feature of this garden. He liked the idea and I went ahead with the design, planted the garden and kept it under my care for several weeks to ensure that all the trees and plants were well settled before the garden went to the West Country. It was delivered to his home a few weeks before the official opening and was on display in his front garden, during which time the donations to his wishing well increased for many people came especially to see the new garden, which had been much publicised.

Plate 14 illustrates the great interest which the miniature trees and plants aroused in two young visitors – who had never seen them before.

Many years ago I was commissioned by a retired nursing sister to make a garden for her to present to a children's hospital. As many of the children were seldom able to leave their beds – except for special treatment – the idea was to have a garden on a trolley. This would be on the terrace most of the time, where it could be seen by patients near the windows but could also be wheeled around the wards for the children in bed to see. I was told that these little tours of the garden were something which the children looked forward to and they were able to notice the development of the plants; the opening of a rose bud, or a miniature daffodil with anticipation and real interest. Because this garden was outdoors most of the time it was possible to have a fairly wide range of plants to flower at different times of the year.

These are only a few instances of how miniature gardens can be adapted to suit the special conditions of the disabled either for individuals or groups.

There are, unfortunately, many disabled people who cannot have a garden out of doors or even a window garden, and for them Chapters 7 and 8 on indoor gardens should be helpful.

I do know that some people, confined to the house, are

also handicapped by being unable to lift anything except the smallest and lightest containers. This difficulty can be overcome by having a series of small plastic bowls or dishes. The owner could then have a miniature tree in one, roses in another, and a few of the plants, listed in Chapter 7, in the third. If these containers are square, or rectangular, they can be arranged to give the impression of one complete landscape, but each little container can be lifted for attention.

7

INDOOR GARDENS

To create and tend a little garden can be a source of endless pleasure especially to those who cannot go out into the open or do much active work. Apart from those physically handicapped in any way there are many able bodied people who live in flats without even an outside window-ledge, yet feel the urge to grow these miniature plants. To those people – young and old – the interest of watching their own plants grow and develop – even in the most limited way – is really stimulating.

The keen rose grower, deprived of a full scale rose garden, can recapture his delight in the equally perfect, but minute rose bushes, as they put forth their new spring foliage and form their tiny buds, to flower most generously for about six months in the year; even when not in flower these little rose bushes have a charm of their own. As related in Chapter 9 these miniature roses were grown originally as indoor pot plants in a Swiss village. Apparently every family in the village had their own group of miniature roses and they have proved ideal plants for indoor culture in other countries.

The best position for an indoor garden is on the window-ledge, preferably one where the light is not obscured by net or nylon curtains. It can be planted in a pottery bowl, or a seed-pan; these are now mass produced in plastic as well as pottery. A specially made trough of very thin section concrete or a glass-fibre trough, as shown in plate 15, can also be planted with subjects suitable for indoor culture; both these types are light in weight and portable. It is important that whatever type of container is used for an indoor garden it should have drainage holes, and unless the window-ledge is tiled it is advisable to have a tray or cork mat to take any moisture which might seep through.

Most alpines, natives of mountainous regions, need direct light above them and so will not flourish indoors; but some trees and plants will tolerate conditions in a living-room, if given some extra attention. It is not generally appreciated that glass itself reduces the light, and it is only in the area quite close to the window that the plants have sufficient light, for their well being. Although the difference may not be noticeable to anyone reading several feet away from the window, such a distance would have a detrimental effect on the plants. The reaction is usually shown by their becoming attenuated and pallid, and the flower buds seldom develop.

I once found some plants which had grown more than twice their normal height and the foliage was a sickly yellowish green. The owner – when she placed the order – assured me that it was to be in a sunny window ' . . . with all the light it is possible to have indoors'. She was quite oblivious to the fact that a tall adjacent building was depriving her garden of the light which it needed. Due to this obstruction the garden was in a position the equivalent of 4ft or 5ft away from the glass. Another small garden was on a stool about 12in *below* the window-ledge. The owner noticed that the plants were elongated and had even staked some of them – laboriously tying the drooping leaves to little sticks – instead of lifting the garden up to the light.

If there is a frame or suitable space available outdoors and it is possible to have two portable gardens – keeping one indoors and changing them over if and when the one indoors shows signs of suffering from insufficient light – then this should be done before the plants begin to lose their compact habit and become pallid and elongated. During the change-over the plants can recuperate in the better light. It is undesirable to make the change too drastic by taking the garden from the living-room and putting it out into scorching sunlight or – even worse – from a warm living-room on a frosty day.

With this arrangement a much wider range of trees and plants can be considered and experiments will prove which plants will be the most rewarding for these special conditions. Some campanulas, asperulas, drabas, cassiopes, primulas, saxifraga and sempervivums will usually respond favourably to this treatment.

If conditions make it impossible to have two gardens or more and change them over for a resting period, or even to put one garden out in top light at frequent intervals, then it would be wiser to limit the selection of plants for indoor culture to those which will withstand lack of direct light and avoid those marked with a * in the list later in this chapter, for these should only be used in more favourable conditions, but it is a matter of personal choice and of experiment.

A long window-box gives much more scope than a bowl or

Fig 13

seed-tray, but it must be regarded as a permanent fixture; the trees and plants selected to suit these conditions, and the garden given a little more attention than one which can be put out into the open occasionally.

Sometimes an architect makes provision for a window garden by designing a recessed trough beneath the window. The trough is lined with concrete and fitted with an outlet pipe leading to an outside drain to carry away any excess water. One such trough is shown in fig 13; the top of the trough was framed with unglazed tiles, so that water could be splashed without doing any harm to what is usually paint-work. This sunken container was most attractive when planted, as the complete little landscape had no visible trough to distract the eye from the garden and the tiled surround made a pleasant frame for this. At the far end was a *Chamaecyparis obtusa* 'Nana', a semi-pendulous tree near the pond, which contains *Hydrocharis morsus-ranae*, with *Acorus gramineus* 'Pusillus'; *Asplenium trichomanes* and *Blechnum penna-marina* near the water's edge and some small carpeting plants to overhang the tiles. There were also several different varieties of miniature roses.

The actual planting of an indoor garden is just the same procedure as described on page 39, but it is of the utmost importance to start with sturdy healthy plants to enable them to withstand the somewhat adverse conditions of indoor culture.

Some of the slow-growing conifers are excellent for indoor gardens and one or more of these will make all the difference to the little landscape, giving height and character as well as a sense of proportion. Unfortunately, most of the junipers and piceas will not tolerate shade; they have a tendency to lose their compact habit of growth and also are susceptible to red-spider mite, which flourishes in the warmth of a living-room. Happily, most of the *chamaecyparis* are satisfactory; I have found *Chamaecyparis pisifera* 'Squarrosa Cyano-viridis' (Boulevard) improves in colour and turns a beautiful blue-grey in shady conditions. Another with silvery blue foliage is *Chamaecyparis pisifera* 'Squarrosa Intermedia', which is more open in habit. Two conifers of rich dark-green foliage are *C. obtusa* 'Nana' and *C. obtusa* 'Nana Kosteri', *C. pisifera* 'Plumosa Compressa', and *C. thyoides* 'Andelyensis Nana', of a lighter green, are all suitable for indoor culture.

Apart from the miniature roses, all of which can be grown indoors, there are a few flowering shrubs which can also add variety and interest. Amongst the best of these are *Cassiope tetragona, Crassula sarcocaulis, Jasminum parkeri, Ulmus parvifolia* var. 'Chessins' and *Zelkova nivea.* Any of the following plants can be grown indoors, but those marked with an asterisk should only be included in gardens which can be put out into the open periodically; to have sufficient light to encourage flowering and to retain their compact habit of growth : —

Acorus gramineus 'Pusillus'
**Anagallis tenella*
Arenaria balearica
**Asperula gussoni*
**A. suberosa*
Asplenium ruta-muraria
A. trichomanes
**Calceolaria tenella*
Centaurium portense
Crassula bolussi
**Erodium chamaedryoides* 'Roseum'
Helxine soleirolii, 'Golden Queen'
H. soleirolii, 'Silver Queen'
Hypericum anagalloides
Laurentia tenella
Mentha requienii
**Rhodohypoxis baurii*
Sedum humifusum
Selaginella apus
S. helvetica

S. helvetica, 'Aurea'
*Viola hederacea,
full descriptions of these will be found in Chapter 10.

Care of indoor gardens does involve more attention than for those grown in the open, but the study of their requirements adds to the interest of ownership. It is extremely important to remember that plants grown indoors lack the benefit of natural moisture in the air, the dew which refreshes the plants even if there has been no rain. Plants give off moisture through their leaves and in an artificially dry atmosphere – especially in a room with gas or central-heating – they give off more than they can spare and subsequently go flabby, sometimes collapsing entirely. To compensate for the unnatural conditions to which the plants are subjected, it is advisable to damp the foliage, using a spray with a fine nozzle filled with tepid water. Spraying should be done at least once a day in hot weather, even twice a day might be necessary if the room is kept at a high temperature. This treatment will also wash off any fine particles of dust which may not be noticeable, but are harmful, as plants breathe through their leaves. Another advantage of this treatment is that it discourages red-spider mite, which breeds more quickly than ever in hot dry conditions.

The damping of the foliage which is to compensate for the dry atmosphere in a warm room, must not be confused with the watering of the roots, which is an entirely different, but essential, operation. This should also be with tepid water, preferably using a can with a fine rose. It is wiser to water generously several times a week to ensure that the water gets down to the roots. If only the top of the soil is watered the moisture may evaporate before it reaches the roots of the plants. How much and how often to water depends on the size of the garden, the temperature of the room in which it is kept, and the condition of the plants – if they are growing and coming into flower or resting. If the latter they will need less water, but if they are coming into flower then they must be watered generously, but never so much that the soil becomes waterlogged.

It is essential to give the plants the maximum light, but if on a really hot day the sun should be beating down on the glass it is advisable to move the garden away from the glass until the danger of scorch has passed. This is simple in the case of a small portable garden, but if a long window garden which is a fixture has to be protected from scorch, an open window will ensure that the plants cannot be affected by the sun through the glass. Conversely, in winter it is inadvisable to leave the garden close to the window at night where there is danger of frost, especially if the room heating is turned off. A large garden can be protected by a piece of polythene at night.

It is extremely important to examine the trees and plants regularly – especially the roses – in case they are attacked by insect pests or mildew. The latter appears on roses subjected to sudden changes of temperature. These afflictions must be dealt with as soon as they are identified.

The above notes are especially important for indoor gardens, but information on any other routine work – such as weeding, lifting and dividing or pruning – will be found in chapter 5.

In some old houses there is a conservatory leading off from the drawing room and, if the staging is reasonably well supported it lends itself to planting a complete landscape, using the whole length of the staging (fig 14). Before embarking on this project the owner should ascertain that there is ample ventilation and also be prepared to provide shading if there should be a hot summer. Although most alpines need top light, they will not tolerate scorching through glass. Apart from these two provisos the possibilities of a landscape which would cover a large area, at a convenient height, are so wide that the owner could have the most wonderful time planning and carrying out such a scheme. There is hardly any limit to the scope of such a garden and the great pleasure it would provide in all weathers.

In old greenhouses the staging is usually constructed of slats of timber with spaces between, so it would be necessary to cover these. Flat or corrugated asbestos would be suitable, but there should be a few drainage holes. The front and each end should have a wall of weathered timber, 4in to 6in high, to contain the drainage material and compost. Then the planting could be carried out as though for a large trough. If there are shelves on the other side a range of small gardens in bowls could be displayed on them.

Although this would be an indoor garden in the sense that the gardener would be protected in all weathers, the choice of plants need not be restricted to those listed for gardens

Fig 14

73

in a room, as they would have light above them. They could, in fact, be any of the plants described in this book.

It might seem to the reader that I have over-stressed the importance of the plants being close to the light of the window; but it is essential to emphasise the difference between some alpines – which will tolerate a little shade – and those usually classed as house plants which can be grown far away from the light.

If, because a suitable position close to the light is not possible and the owner has not the time to attend to the garden as outlined, then a good alternative is a Fern Case, which does not need direct light or much attention. These are more fully described in the next chapter.

8

FERN CASES AND GARDENS
UNDER GLASS DOMES

The great advantage of this form of gardening is that, protected by the glass, the plants will not suffer in a centrally heated room where the hot, dry atmosphere is detrimental to most plants. This makes fern cases especially valuable to invalids and elderly people who are confined to the house; also, to anyone who is active, but has to be away from home frequently and could not cope with any other form of garden. Once properly planted and well balanced these gardens can be left for fairly long periods without any attention. In the shelter of a glass case the plants are not affected by smoke, dust, draughts or fluctuating temperatures and, as they flourish in semi-shade, they can be placed anywhere in the room away from the window.

They are entirely different from bottle gardens which are usually planted in carboys, cider flagons, or other bottles with narrow necks and are difficult to plant; it is even more difficult to give the plants any attention they may require. Because of this they are sometimes neglected after the first interest has waned; then the plants become overcrowded or unhealthy and the glass green with *algae*.

A fern case, like a miniature conservatory, fitted with either a hinged or detachable door gives easy access to the plants and so eliminates the unhappy conditions so often prevalent in bottle gardens. The owner of a fern case, or garden under a glass dome, can easily attend to cutting back, weeding, lifting or dividing when necessary. Also, some flowering plants can be included as it is easy to cut off faded blooms, which if left in a narrow-necked carboy or bottle garden are unsightly and might develop botrytis.

Fern cases were extremely popular in Victorian times. Their development by Dr Ward was unexpected, but also interesting because he was very anxious to grow ferns in his garden and was defeated by the dirty atmosphere in his area near the London docks. He was a keen naturalist and wishing to observe the emergence of a Sphinx moth from the chrysalis, he buried the latter in a bottle filled with moist earth and kept the lid tightly closed. He looked at the bottle every day and noticed that the vapour rising from the earth was condensed on the inner surface of the glass, trickled down the sides of the bottle, and so kept a uniform degree of humidity within it.

About a week before the expected change of the insect Dr Ward was astonished to see a seedling fern growing in the bottle. The spontaneous growth of one of the species he had tried unsuccessfully to grow in his garden gave him new ideas. He pondered seriously on the conditions necessary for their well-being. From his observation of the fern growing sturdily in the bottle, he deduced that these plants needed still air, consistent moisture and semi-shade, as well as freedom from dust and soot. In order to prove his theory he allowed the fern to remain in the bottle, where it grew and flourished for nearly four years. During this time the cover was not removed and so no water was added. In his book, *Growth of Plants in Closely Glazed Cases*, Dr Ward does not mention the fate of the moth!

During the four years Dr Ward carried out many experiments in bottles of various sizes, and then developed glazed cases in which he grew a wide range of plants. One of his most important and spectacular triumphs was the Killarney Fern, *Trichomanes speciosum*. This is a plant of delicate beauty, which grows in caves and near waterfalls where the atmosphere is consistently moist. The foliage is so thin that it shrivels without humidity and was considered most difficult to cultivate, but it grew and flourished in his glazed case.

76

Fig 15

Subsequently such cases, known as Wardian Cases (fig 15), became very fashionable and were made in many different styles and sizes, varying from those which were small enough to stand on a drawing-room table to others made especially to fit in a recess. Some were of the simplest box shape, whilst others had a span roof or domed top; many had elaborate ornamentation. To quote from a book of the period: 'These are elegant and pleasing additions to the most tasteful and elaborately furnished drawing-room, whilst some of the more common rustic forms may serve the purpose equally well in the modest sitting room of the City Clerk or artisan.'

Such elaborate designs as the Victorian fern case would be far too costly to reproduce now, but a simple modern version as shown in plate 18 could be made. The base is a black plastic tray, the frame of metal is glazed, puttied as in an aquarium. The angle of the roof is most important, to encourage the condensed moisture to run down into the earth. To have the best view, the highest side should be at the front. With a flat top as used on an aquarium tank the moisture tends to gather in blobs and drip on to the foliage, in which case it is necessary to lift the top and wipe it, this of course reduces the humidity so it might be desirable to syringe the plants gently to compensate for the reduction of moisture. When planning the structure of the smaller case the glazed top should not be too heavy to lift; the larger type should be fitted with a door, giving easy access to the plants.

A shallow round bowl planted with ferns, smaller selaginellas and mosses, covered with a glass dome will look charming. Suitable glass domes can sometimes be found in antique shops. It is extremely important that whatever the type – fern case or dish covered with a bell globe – for the glass to fit closely *within* the rim of the container, so that there is no gap which would allow the soil to dry out. Some people, not realising that the moisture must be conserved, have used glass covers which are either too small, or – even worse – too large. In the latter case the condensed moisture runs down outside the plant container and is wasted.

There are many ferns and selaginellas (a family of plants even more delicate and lacy than ferns, but not as well known as they should be) which are beautiful, almost ethereal in form and colour, ranging from vivid gold to rich green. As the latter is the most restful of colours these plants are of therapeutic value to people who are tired or ill. The cases can be quite small and portable or on a more ambitious scale, built especially to occupy a recess or alcove in a hall or on a landing.

For anyone who has a lean-to greenhouse or conservatory the same scheme can be carried out using the whole length, or part of, the staging, making a superb landscape with various ferns and selaginellas, and some shade-loving flowering plants which enjoy humid conditions. To carry out this scheme successfully it is important that the roof of the greenhouse should be shaded. I made one such fern case in a small green-house, which had a base of corrugated asbestos, with a 6in retaining frontage of wood treated with a preservative. The back and roof were of plastic, coloured a soft blue-green to make an effective background, against which the delicate silhouettes of the ferns and selaginellas were clearly defined. The front, higher than the back, was of clear plastic and divided into two sections (as the whole case is 6ft long).

When the structure was finished, the grooves in the asbestos base were filled with pieces of broken flower-pot, washed to ensure that no pests were introduced and mixed with a few pieces of charcoal. Above this was a layer of peat and then the compost (half loam, half peat mixed with fine grit and charcoal, the latter to keep the soil from becoming sour) arranged higher at the back and undulating to the level of the retaining wall in the foreground.

An irregular-shaped pool, which adds humidity to the atmosphere and is decorative, was first positioned. Then some rocks of interesting shapes and varying heights were placed at irregular intervals, and the whole area thoroughly watered and

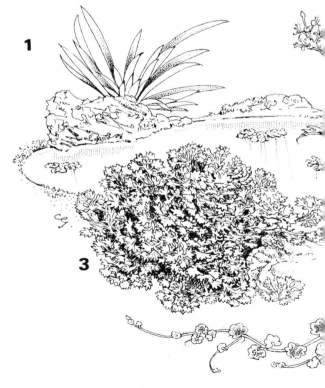

Fig 16 1 *Acorus gramineus*
        3 *Selaginella apus*

2

4

2 *Astilbe glaberrima 'Saxosa'*
4 *Sibthorpia europaea 'Variegata'*

Fig 17   *Hymenophyllum wilsoni*

left to settle for a few days before planting. To give the illusion of distance, the taller ferns and selaginellas were grouped at the back.

In the centre, quite close to the pool, a large specimen of *Trichomanes speciosum* was planted to have the benefit of the moist atmosphere, and nearby a patch of the very tiny *Hymenophyllum wilsoni* (fig 17) made a striking contrast. To surround the pool *Blechnum penna-marina* and *Acorus gramineus* 'Pusillus' were planted; both of these flourished as waterside plants and the latter also on a little island in the pool.

In a tank, 24in x 12in x 12in – originally an aquarium – covered with a sheet of glass, we grew some flowering plants as well as ferns; the glass was lifted and wiped whenever drops of water accumulated on the flat surface to prevent them dropping in blobs on the plants. Apart from the ferns, *Anagallis tenella*, *Rhodohypoxis baurii* and *Astilbe glaberrima* 'Saxosa' were grown. The first two flowered generously over a long period and although the astilbe had a shorter flowering time, it grew happily in the moist atmosphere and the dark fern-like foliage made a splendid contrast beside *Sibthorpia europaea* 'Variegata', which is a very pale silvery green.

In his book, Dr Ward describes his experiments with many

other flowering plants which he grew successfully in his fern cases of many different sizes, which he kept in various parts of the house. The reader may be interested in trying plants, other than those mentioned above, according to what is available locally, especially those which enjoy shade and a moist atmosphere. Some of the best non-flowering plants which are known to flourish in fern cases are:—*Acorus gramineus* 'Pusillus', *Adiantum capillus* 'Veneris', *A. pedatum, Asplenium trichomanes, Blechnum penna-marina, Ceterach officinarum, Hymenophyllum wilsoni, Polypodium vulgare, Polystichum setiferum* 'Divisilobum Densum', *Scolopendrium vulgare, Selaginella emiliana, S. emiliana* 'Aurea', *S. martensii, S. serpens, Trichomanes speciosum* (The Killarney Fern) and of course any mosses which are available, as most of these improve in a fern case and are wondrously beautiful when seen in detail.

The golden age of plant hunters was long before the days of air transport and we, of this century, owe our thanks to Dr Ward, not only for his introduction of fern cases, but also because his glazed cases enabled plant hunters – who risked so much to collect new plants – to reduce the heavy losses which were inevitable when the plants were packed in crates for long sea voyages. I am happy to conclude this chapter with a dedication from a much valued book, over a hundred

Fig 18   Common cord moss

and thirty years old, *British Ferns*, by Thomas Moore, FLS.

To
N. B. Ward, Esq., FLS,
whose invention of
CLOSE GLAZED CASES
has extended the cultivation of ferns to the parlour,
the window-sill, and the city court-yard
as well as enriched our gardens with the fruits and flowers
of other lands
THIS LITTLE VOLUME
is, with much respect and esteem, dedicated
by his obliged friend,
THE AUTHOR, Thomas Moore, FLS, 1851.

9

TREES, SHRUBS, AND ROSES

The trees and shrubs described in the following pages are only a few of the many which are suitable for trough gardens, and are selected from those which have given me the most pleasure; to extend these lists and descriptions would seem more like a catalogue, but the reader will find many other conifers and plants at various nurseries. Anyone not familiar with their botanical names invariably protests, perhaps with some justification, because it does seem that the smaller the plant the longer the name, especially if it has several synonyms. For instance, the Cheddar Pink which used to be called *Dianthus caesius* is now burdened with the name of *D. gratianopolitanus*. Unfortunately, these names are unavoidable, as they are botanically correct and local names are sometimes misleading. An example of this is the engaging pink rhododendron, *R. ferrugineum*, known locally in Switzerland as *'alpenrose'* (the 'alpine rose'); and in England *Scilla nutans* is known as a bluebell, whereas in Scotland the bluebell is the delightful *Campanula rotundifolia*, known in England as the wild harebell. Once you are familiar with the conifer and alpine plant names they will come just as easily as delphinium, chrysanthemum or rhododendron, which are so much in common use that many people think they are English, but they are international, usually derived from Latin or Greek. Anyone wishing to order a plant from a nursery would generally find it listed in the catalogue under its botanical name.

It is advisable to purchase a pot grown plant from a specialist rather than hoping to collect some plants from their native habitats. Plant hunting was unlimited in the days when wild plants were not protected, but in these days collecting should not be done without a permit. Unfortunately, these regulations do not always have the desired effect. Some rare plants have been lost by 'progress' in various districts – building motorways or reservoirs – so perhaps if anyone who is capable of looking after a rare treasure which is in danger does collect a few specimens they may be forgiven, provided they do care for them and so ensure that the plant is not lost to posterity.

When purchasing a plant it is really wiser to select young pot grown specimens because, as Farrer says ' . . . those gardeners who put things in on Monday and expect to have their eyes filled with Glory by Wednesday are apt to be disappointed'. Conversely, anyone who goes to a flower show or a garden centre and purchases a pot plant in full flower – with the same expectations – will probably find that in three days time the flowers are over and the plant has wilted, as they are usually at their peak when exhibited.

Miniature trees are really fascinating, and very few people can resist the charm of a tree which looks natural and mature, even ancient, although only a few inches high. The trees are the most important feature of the garden; they are handsome at all times of the year and their diversity of shape will give character to the simplest design. Some are flat-topped and spreading, others dome-shaped or conical, some pendulous and the slender spire of *Juniperus communis* 'Compressa', like a miniature poplar, is always impressive.

Although referred to as evergreen, these conifers are far from monotonous. Their colours range from the palest to the darkest rich green, from delicate gold to dull bronze, from grey-green to metallic silver or steel blue. There are some, especially cryptomerias and thujas, which change their colour in winter and this makes them even more interesting and attractive, whilst the delicate green of the emerging spring foliage is most spectacular on the piceas.

Unlike the Japanese trees, known as Bonsai, which are

artificially stunted by pruning of the roots and branches and also by confining the roots in small containers, the trees, mostly conifers, described in this book have a naturally slow rate of growth, sometimes no more than a $\frac{1}{4}$in a year. Because they are so slow-growing, they can reach a great age whilst retaining a truly miniature form. Although they are usually grown in pots – for sale in nurseries – which may restrict the growth to a certain extent, they do not 'bolt' when transplanted into a trough or the open ground, and the difference in rate of growth is almost imperceptible. Most of them can be relied upon to remain in proportion with the alpines in a trough garden for five to fifteen years or more. The difference is of course governed by the type of tree in question. I have a *Chamaecyparis obtusa* 'Nana' in a stone sink which was originally pot grown, but has been in that trough for about twenty years; it is now over forty years old and has shown no difference in the rate of growth since being transplanted from the pot to the trough.

Some of those suitable for trough gardens, or landscapes on a slightly larger scale can be selected from a wide range of miniature evergreen conifers. The word 'selected' must be emphasised because there are conifers classed as 'dwarf' by some growers which will reach a height of 6ft or more, as they are related to some of the same species which grow up to 30ft or 40ft and so, in comparison, are 'dwarf', but these do not come within the scope of this book. There are many others with a truly slow rate of growth which will not reach 2ft in twenty or thirty years and can be used in a trough garden for a very long time, whilst others – the best of all – have such an extremely slow rate of growth that they can be left in a trough indefinitely.

Quite often some dwarf conifers are described in books and catalogues as 'bun-shaped' and grown to suit this unfortunate description; that is, planted so deeply that the trunk is submerged and much of the beauty of the tree is lost. I have found that by taking a young specimen which has been treated in this fashion and occasionally repotting, each time revealing a little more of the trunk, will improve it and transform the 'bun' into a tree. Many share my opinion that a tree without a trunk is more like a bush than a real tree in miniature.

The true miniature conifers have originated either from (*a*) seedlings or (*b*) sports.

(*a*) Some have developed from seedlings which germinated on a rocky mountain-side, where the austere conditions have induced a stunted growth and very much reduced the tree in all its parts. Cuttings taken from these seedlings generally reproduce the compact habit of the parent tree, but sometimes a cutting when grown in less harsh conditions will revert to a coarser habit of growth. Others have been propagated (by cuttings) from seedling trees which have been found in private

Plate 15 top
A garden in a glass fibre container, 20in x 9in, with *Picea mariana* 'Nana', *Salix boydii*, *Saxifraga* Faldonside, *Calceolaria tenella*, *Rosa* Elf, *Sempervivum arenarium* and *Ionopsideum acaule*. March. A portable garden suitable for conditions where it could be indoors for short periods and then have a recuperative time in a frame or greenhouse

Plate 16 bottom left
Glass fibre reproduction of antique vase covered with a glass dome, fitting just inside the rim, with *Adiantum pedatum*, *Blechnum penna-marina*, *Selaginella martensii*, and *S. emiliana* 'Aurea'

Plate 17 centre right
White plastic tray, 16in x 9in, with *Chamaecyparis pisifera* 'Plumosa Compressa' and *Crassula sarcocaulis*, *Rosa* Elf, *Erodium chamaedryoides* 'Roseum', *Hypericum anagalloides* and *Helxine soleirolii* 'Golden Queen' and *H. soleirolii* 'Silver Queen'. June

Plate 18 bottom right
Modern type of fern case with a glazed metal frame, higher at the front than the back to give the best view, fitting closely within a plastic tray; planted with *Adiantum pedatum*, *A. capillus* 'Veneris', *Selaginella martensii* 'Variegata'. A small pool with *Acorus gramineus* 'Pusillus' and *Blechnum penna-marina* nearby

gardens or nurseries where large conifers were grown, and these particular seedlings have – for no reason as yet understood – persisted in a slow rate of growth, retaining on a very small scale all the characteristics of the parent tree. A good example is to be seen in plate 7.

(b) Those which have been developed from a sport or mutation, generally in the form of a 'witches' broom'. This is a congested mass of small branchlets and foliage which grows out of a branch of a full-scale tree but remains in a tight cluster of foliage, much smaller and more dense than on the normal branches, in the form of a complete miniature tree. Cuttings from these mutations will generally reproduce the same compact habit and reduced size of leaf and branchlet.

Fig 19 shows the 'witches' broom' which was found on a *Cryptomeria japonica* 150ft high. The miniature tree grew into a perfect replica out of a branch 16ft above ground-level.

Another method of producing miniature trees is by grafting. There are some conifers which are extremely difficult to propagate by cuttings, and grafting is the only method by which they can be reproduced. This is generally used for pinus and cedrus and in some cases chamaecyparis. As the latter come fairly easily from cuttings, it is usually the large

Plate 19 top
Concrete trough, 36in x 24in, designed as a rose garden with pergolas, trellis and rose beds as near as possible a replica of the full scale rose garden which the owner had to leave. The paths radiating from the central ornament sloped down to a lower level. The two conifers are *Chamaecyparis obtusa* 'Nana'

Plate 20 bottom
Concrete trough, 36in x 24in. The decorative background was painted white, the central path leading to a silver Grecian figurine. The paths dividing the rose beds edged with *Saxifraga aizoon* 'Baldensis', each bed planted with a different variety of miniature roses, totalling fifty rose bushes. The conifers, *Juniperus communis* 'Compressa', being young specimens are still rather open in habit; the *Chamaecyparis obtusa* 'Nana' are roughly the same age. The birds in the foreground are of carved bone and weatherproof

Fig 19

commercial grower who uses this method because it is possible to produce a fair-sized saleable tree in much less time than by cuttings. It has been stated that grafted trees tend to revert and cease to be the neat compact conifer one expects; like so many generalisations this is only partly true. I have some handsome grafted trees which have not deviated from their close habit of growth over a period of ten to twenty years. Of course there are some which have grown more rapidly than others, but I think this depends upon the material used. Obviously if rather open coarse foliage is selected to produce a large saleable tree in less time than it would take to grow one with fine compact foliage, the result will be a much coarser tree. Also, cuttings taken from the main stem of a conifer may produce trees which are entirely different from others taken from the lateral branches of the same tree. There is frequently considerable variation in the size of the leaves and branchlets, between different specimens bearing the same name, especially in *Chamaecyparis obtusa* 'Nana'. Also, much depends on the stock upon which the scion is grafted as this may influence the rate of growth.

Before planting, or even purchasing a conifer, it is advantageous to be able to assess approximately, what it will look like in three, five or ten years' time. This is especially important when a very young one is under consideration. The rate of growth and colour of the foliage is sometimes affected by the soil and position in which the conifer is grown. Generally the colour improves when the tree is in semi-shade. This is especially noticeable when the tree is of glaucous foliage. These conifers require a good peaty soil and adequate drainage, for they must never be waterlogged, but even more important they must never be allowed to become too dry.

When considering the selection of a tree, or trees, the following brief descriptions may be helpful. They are divided into three groups, but even so this grouping depends upon the size and age of the tree when transplanted.

(a) Those which are very slow-growing and can be left in

a trough garden indefinitely, but may need a little top dressing occasionally;

(b) those not likely to outgrow the sink in less than ten years;

(c) those which, although attractive, are more vigorous in growth and may have to be moved within five to six years.

For the patient gardener a slow-growing conifer (a) will give more lasting pleasure. For the temperament eager for an immediate effect even a fair-sized specimen of those marked (c) will be satisfactory for a few years.

All the above figures are based on the assumption that any tree selected is quite a young specimen.

Conifers

ABIES

A. balsamea 'Hudsonia' has leaves which are somewhat larger than those of the other conifers described in this book; their size and the way they grow on the branch, make this a quite distinctive conifer. The leaves, about $\frac{1}{2}$in long, and slender, are slightly curved growing at right-angles from either side of the mid-rib. It is not until it is about eight to ten years old that it develops its unusual character. (b)

A. lasiocarpa 'Compacta' is an arresting conifer of striking silvery-blue foliage and broadly conical habit. The garden in plate 4 shows a good specimen with the new spring growth just emerging. (c)

CHAMAECYPARIS (Dwarf Cypress)

There is a wide range of these, varying considerably in habit, rate of growth and colour of foliage. Some of the best are:

C. lawsoniana 'Ellwoodii' forms a dense column of glaucous foliage. It is a good tree for a beginner and is quite effective in a trough garden for a limited time if a young specimen is used. (c)

C. lawsoniana 'Lutea Nana' is fairly slow-growing, with flattish branches and foliage of a rich golden yellow. It forms a conical bushy shape and is of value for colour, rather than contour, to make a contrast with a dark tree. (b)

C. obtusa 'Filicoides' is an unusual and graceful conifer with widely spaced, arching branches. The dark green flattish leaves grow at right-angles on both sides of the branchlet, arranged like the fronds of a fern, hence its English name 'fern cypress' (plate 9). (b)

C. obtusa 'Nana' is one of the most attractive and one of the most popular conifers with its sturdy trunk and fan-shaped branchlets which curve upwards in tiers on spreading branches. The foliage of a well-grown specimen is a rich dark green. Some are dense, compact and slow-growing and would be classed as (*a*); others are similar in structure and habit, but so much more open and coarse that they will attain twice, or even three times the size of the foregoing and would be (*b*) or even (c) (plates 3, 7, 10, 13 and 19).

C. obtusa 'Nana Kosteri' is one of the most handsome of this group, even more attractive than the above. It has a similar sturdy trunk and spreading branches, but the fan-shaped branchlets curve downwards in a graceful sweep. A mature tree, up to 12in to 15in high, shows tier upon tier of these branchlets, forming a most decorative pattern. A well-grown specimen gives the impression of a really ancient tree (plates 1 and 12). (b)

C. obtusa 'Pygmaea' is a flat-topped spreading tree of rather open habit, with semi-pendulous branchlets usually a rich bronze green. A good subject to plant beside a pool (plate 11). (a)

C. pisifera 'Nana' is more bushy in habit and is seldom grown with a trunk, usually several stems clothed with dense branchlets of foliage, dark blue-green above and silvery on the under surface. Sometimes a young specimen with a single stem can be selected and this will grow into a much more attractive tree-like shape (plate 8). (b)

C. pisifera 'Nana Variegata' is similar to the above, but the branchlets are flecked with creamy-yellow at the tips. (b)

C. pisifera 'Plumosa Compressa' is bushy in habit, with

numerous branches which rise almost vertically from the ground, with dense moss-like foliage varying from golden-bronze green in full sun to a soft glaucous green in shade. It is more compact and slow-growing than most conifers, seldom exceeding 8in to 10in. Young specimens can be used in the smallest gardens with some of the tiniest alpines (plate 17). (a)

C. pisifera 'Squarrosa Cyano-viridis' (Boulevard) is a rather unusual tree forming a pyramid of ascending branches clothed with slender leaves which are a most wonderful colour – almost blue, shot with grey-green. The colour improves if it is grown in semi-shade. (b)

C. pisifera 'Squarrosa Intermedia' also improves in colour when grown in semi-shade. It is dense, dome-shaped in habit with branchlets of fine blue-grey foliage. This is one of the few conifers which can be pruned, as it occasionally produces long terminal shoots which spoil its appearance and these can be trimmed to maintain a good shape. (c)

C. thyoides 'Andelyensis Nana' is very slow-growing with ascending branches which form a symmetrical cone of delicate moss-like foliage of dark green. In the early spring microscopic flowers of brilliant red appear on the tips of the foliage and in the autumn tiny cones develop on the more mature trees plate 13). (a)

CRYPTOMERIA

C. japonica 'Nana' (syn: 'Pygmaea') grows erect, with a sturdy trunk, spreading semi-pendulous branches rather widely spaced. The foliage is a light green with a tinge of bronze in the winter. (b)

C. japonica 'Vilmoriniana' is dense in habit and variable in contour, with ascending branches. The leaves are thick and stiff, a brilliant grass-green in the spring, turning russet brown in autumn and winter. (b)

JUNIPERUS

J. communis 'Compressa' is undoubtedly another of the most popular of all dwarf conifers. It grows in an erect slender spire and is most effective when planted in pairs in a formal garden. Very young specimens are rather sparse and open. It is only when they reach eight to ten years of age that they become dense and shapely, and when over twenty years they achieve a sleek symmetrical elegance which is unique (plates 1, 3, 7, 12 and 20). (a)

J. recurva 'Coxii' (The Chinese Weeping Juniper) although not a true miniature, a young specimen can be used in a trough garden for several years before it grows too large for the scale of the garden. Its graceful weeping habit makes this an ideal conifer for overhanging a pool. Young plants may need staking and possibly some of the lower branches may also need support, but when well-trained this can be a most beautiful tree. (b)

J. recurva 'Viridis' is similar in habit, but the foliage is finer, as the slender leaves are smaller and grow more closely together. (b)

J. squamata 'Glassell' has a sturdy trunk with rather stiff ascending branches, triangular in shape, at varying angles to the trunk, giving a windswept effect. The branchlets are pendulous, the foliage a bright grass-green and it often bears a profusion of minute cones. This is quite a distinct form, splendid for a rocky trough garden. (b)

J. squamata 'Pygmaea' is a semi-prostrate conifer which is very slow-growing. The small leaves are a soft glaucous green and it is a particularly charming little tree for trailing over a rock or the sides of a trough. (a)

PICEA (Spruce)
A large group, most of which have a spectacular transformation from the dark green of the mature foliage to the pale green of the new growth in the spring. A few of the best for trough gardens are:

P. abies 'Nidiformis' forms a dense rounded tree with spreading branches, almost horizontal (plate 6). (b)

P. abies 'Pygmaea' is one of the smallest and most compact of this group, with erect trunk and ascending branches. A gem for small gardens. (a)

P. albertiana 'Conica' grows in a symmetrical cone shape, with bright grass-green foliage and a delightful pine scent. (c)

P. mariana 'Nana' (syn: P. nigra 'Nana') forms a dense dome-shape, which can be greatly improved by discreet pruning of some of the lower branches to reveal the trunk. The foliage is a glaucous green which, in the early spring, has minute crimson tips (plates 5 and 15). (b)

THUJA

T. orientalis 'Rosedalis Compacta' forms an oval-shaped bush with fine foliage which is pale golden-green in the spring, turning glaucous green in the summer and bronze-purple in winter. A splendid tree for a contrast in colour rather than shape. (b)

Broad-Leaved Trees and Shrubs

Acer palmatum 'Dissectum Atropurpureum' (plate 3) is a strikingly handsome maple with spreading branches and finely divided leaves of rich bronze-crimson. This is deciduous, but in winter the bare branches have good lines and the emergence of the young foliage is very lovely and welcome in the spring. They are usually grafted and start from 15in to 18in high,

Fig 20 *Betula nana*

98

and so are only suitable for the larger type of garden. They look magnificent with a background of silver foliage plants.

Betula nana (fig 20) is a true miniature birch tree. The deciduous leaves are rounded, net-veined and deeply notched; in spring the small dark red catkins stand erect. A charming tree which may need pruning to keep it shapely and in proportion. (b)

Cassiope lycopodioides is semi-prostrate; the branches are densely covered with minute stemless leaves overlapping each other in a tight little plait. The reddish-bronze flower stems rise vertically from the leaf axils with single white bell flowers hanging gracefully from them. This exceptionally beautiful plant needs a sheltered position, preferably in lime-free soil in semi-shade. April/May. (a)

C. tetragona is similar in foliage and flowers, but is erect and pyramidal in habit. April/May. (a)

Crassula sarcocaulis has a thick sturdy trunk and ascending branches with small fleshy leaves. The tiny flowers, borne in clusters, are bright pink in the bud, opening out to a paler shade. It is charming, but not entirely hardy and is suitable for indoor culture. (a)

Erica vulgaris 'Foxii Nana' is a compact little heather with dark green foliage and rosy-lilac flowers in August. (a)

Helichrysum selago 'Minor' is a quaint little shrub, like a silvery Club Moss. The ascending branches are densely covered with tiny stemless leaves, overlapping each other in a whipcord effect. The small white 'everlasting' flowers are borne on the tips of the branches in August. (a)

Jasminum parkeri is a true miniature jasmine with stiff branches, small dark green glossy leaves and sweetly scented yellow flowers, which are followed in the autumn by shining-black seed heads. June/July. (a)

Salix. There are numerous dwarf willows, most of which have decorative catkins.

S. x boydii grows erect with gnarled trunk and sturdy branches; the rounded crinkled leaves are a silvery-grey in the spring, turning to a dark metallic grey later in the year. The catkins are inconspicuous. This plant is valued for the foliage and habit of growth, which is so handsome (plate 15). (a)

S. myrsinites 'Jacquiniana' is semi-prostrate. The leaves are narrow, bright green with reddish margins. In the early stages the catkins are bright red (and as they mature the yellow stamens emerge), lasting about two weeks. March / April. (b)

Fig 21   *Salix serpyllifolia*

S. serpyllifolia (fig 21) is prostrate, hugging the ground, with small bright green leaves; microscopic yellow catkins emerge in April / May. (c)

Syringa microphylla is a miniature lilac with ascending branches and roundish leaves, which are deciduous. The sweetly scented rosy-lilac flowers appear in the late spring. (c)

Fig 22   *Ulmas parvifolia*

100

Ulmus parvifolia 'Chessins' (fig 22) is a true miniature elm which is deciduous. The trunk is a pinkish-grey and so are the spreading, sometimes pendulous, branches. The alternate leaves, about $\frac{1}{4}$in long, are characteristic in shape of the full-sized elm, dark glossy-green above and pale grey-green on the under surface. (b)

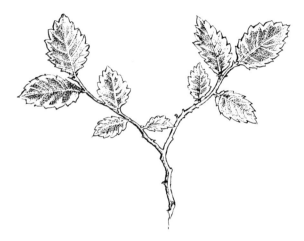

Fig 23   *Zelkova nivea*

Zelkova nivea (fig 23) is similar in habit to the above, but the leaves are slightly larger and are a delicate pale green with a creamy margin, turning a pinkish bronze in the autumn before falling. This is an exceptionally graceful and colourful shrub and the foliage shows up strikingly against the greyish trunk and branches. (b)

Miniature Roses

Of all the trees and plants which grow on a diminutive scale, the true miniature roses seem to me the most wonderful. Although so small they are well-proportioned in leaf, bud and flower and are perfect replicas of full-scale roses. They are

101

enchanting and have a very long flowering season, which for such small plants is really astonishing. Their Lilliputian size suggests that they might be tender, but they are really quite hardy, provided that they have been raised to be grown out of doors and hardened off when transferred from the propagating section. Therefore it is advisable to purchase them from a nursery rather than a florist's shop, unless they are intended for indoor culture.

The original and parent plant, *Rosa Roulettii*, was grown in Switzerland exclusively as an indoor pot plant. It was not until a famous Swiss grower experimented with a small cutting and grew some in the open ground that he discovered that – contrary to local tradition – it was really quite hardy. This discovery was made very many years ago.

One of the most astonishing pictures I have ever seen was on a winter day when the sun was shining on one of my trough gardens, which was completely submerged beneath about 6in of snow. Gradually the contours of the trees were revealed as the snow melted and then a tiny hole appeared in the flat surface of the snow; through this there came a minute pink tip of a rose bud. Gradually the size of the hole increased to about 2in across and in a fairy cave a *Rosa Roulettii* in its entirety could be seen, with every leaf crisp and several minute buds opening out with a shining radiance, as fresh and as lovely as on a day in June. The beauty of this little plant was undoubtedly enhanced by the sparkling snow and the contrasting bluish darkness below (fig 24).

Now there are many different varieties of miniature roses, bred in Holland by de Vink, who used *Roulettii* as one of the parent plants, and these are obtainable from specialist nurseries. A few of the best and smallest are:

'Cinderella' – flowers of pearly white shading to a delicate pink, fully double, borne in clusters of three or four.

'Maid Marion' (syn: 'Red Imp') – fully double, rather flattish flowers of vivid red, which have a long-lasting quality.

'Peon' – semi-double flowers of red with a white centre.

Fig 24   *Rosa Roulettii*

'Pumila' – similar to *Roulettii*, but larger in leaf, bud and flower.

'Red Elf' (usually known as 'Elf') – one of the most beautiful of all the miniature roses. The flowers, borne singly, are of the richest dark red, velvety in texture, with a touch of white at the base of the petals.

'Roulettii' (the original rose found so many years ago in

103

Switzerland) – semi-double flowers, borne singly, with slender buds varying from the palest shell-pink to a deep rose colour. A well-grown plant taken from a small cutting is truly minute.

'Sweet Fairy' – fully double flowers, rather flat with pointed petals of the palest lilac pink. This is one of the few little roses with a strong perfume, which is quite remarkable in such a small plant.

'Yellow Bantam' has buds of rich yellow, opening out to a paler shade, sometimes creamy white. A very pretty rose to grow in contrast with the reds and pinks.

Miniature roses are subject to attacks by insect pests, mildew and/or botrytis. The diameter of the stem of a rosebud is so minute – barely the size of one greenfly – that even one or two of these pests can devastate the plant, so they must be protected by the appropriate insecticide or fungicide (see chapter 5).

Miniature roses can be kept shapely by selective pruning – to just above a node or joint – when cutting off dead flowers; this also encourages the plant to form new buds. Some varieties, especially Maid Marion and Peon, have a tendency to produce coarse basal shoots which are out of character and these should be removed. If the plant has made much vigorous growth during the summer it can be cut back in the late autumn to ensure that it remains compact.

10

ALPINES, ANNUALS, BULBS
AND AQUATICS

Alpines flower in almost all colours, but there are very few reds among the smaller ones, even the mossy saxifraga, and some of the hybrid dianthus, which are good vivid reds, are too exuberant for small trough gardens, but they can be used in gardens on a larger scale. There is a variety of rhodohypoxis, which is a good red, and some of the sempervivum flowers are a dull red; but the foliage of the latter and that of some sedums turn a very rich red if conditions suit them.

Every shade of pink is represented, from the palest of *Anagallis tenella*, to the soft rosy tone of *Saxifraga* x 'Cranbourne', and to the rich pink of *Centaurium portense*. Yellows range from the palest of *Saxifraga burseriana* 'Sulphurea' to the rich golden-yellow of *Narcissus asturiensis* and the lovely lemon-yellow of *Fritillaria citrina*. Blues are scarce but invaluable – from the tiny *Myosotis rupicola* to the glory of the gentians. The purples are represented by soldanellas, primulas and campanulas, from the palest lilac to deep rich violet. In many catalogues campanulas are described as blue, pale blue, rich blue and even 'dainty' blue, which is very misleading to anyone who does not know them, as they are all varying shades of purple or pure white.

The texture of the petals varies from the almost gossamer delicacy of the asperulas to the rich velvet of *Gentiana verna*, *Rhodohypoxis platypetala* has a magnolia-like surface whilst the petals of *Soldanella alpina*, when examined closely, seem to be composed of myriads of microscopic sequins, sparkling and changing in intensity with any variation of light.

Most of the plants described in the following pages – natives of mountainous regions from many different parts of the world – are all small, in varying degrees, and can be roughly divided into five types:

(*a*) those with numerous small leaves on extremely short stalks – or stemless – so densely crowded that they form a dome and are usually known as 'cushion' plants. The flowers, on slender stems, radiate from the dome, as in the Kabschia saxifraga;

(*b*) the more open tuft or rosette, with flower-stems rising from the centre, such as erinus or primula;

(*c*) those which wind their way between the rocks and other plants with flowers rising at frequent intervals, like hypsella and some of the campanulas;

(*d*) the low mat-forming plants which root as they spread, in the habit of the raoulias;

(*e*) those which are prostrate, but spread out from one main root such as linaria, veronica and gypsophila. The latter sometimes roots from the trailing stems, but mostly they spread out from the main root.

There are, of course, many other plants not listed here which are suitable for trough gardens; but I have confined my descriptions to some of those which we have grown and admire, deleting any which are difficult or rare.

There are some plants which are considered hardy and can be expected to go through the winter with fog and periods of excessive rain or snow, and come up as lovely as ever in the spring. But this does not mean that they will all go on indefinitely. Many plants are long-lived, but others will grow happily and flower generously for a few years and then die suddenly for no apparent reason. It is as well to recognise that some such as *Gentiana verna* and *Primula scotica* are usually short-lived.

In the following descriptions the time of flowering and the height of the flowers can only be an approximate guide for environment, as well as the care given to any individual garden, will have an effect on the flowering. Unless particular mention is made of soil or special conditions, which any plant needs, it can be assumed that as far as our experience goes it is not fussy.

ACORUS

A. gramineus 'Pusillus' (fig 16) is a diminutive rush, growing in tufts of slender bright green leaves, 2in high. It is invaluable beside a pool, or even on an island in a pool, as it flourishes in a moist position.

ANAGALLIS

A. tenella (Bog Pimpernel) forms a mat of trailing stems flat on the ground, rooting at frequent intervals, covered with pairs of small rounded leaves on short stalks, the upturned flowers of palest pink are borne singly on slender 1in stems. In shade or semi-shade, and a peaty soil which retains the moisture, it flowers in profusion over a long period in the summer. A plant of fairy-like beauty.

ANDROSACE

A. carnea 'Halleri' has rosettes of slender leaves and clusters of deep pink flowers, 3in high. April/May.

A. sempervivoides grows in rosettes of rounded leaves close to the ground. It increases by stolons and although it takes up more room than the above it is easily controlled if required. The flowers are a brilliant pink borne in clusters on erect 2in stems. April/May.

A. vitaliana (Syn: *Douglasia vitaliana*) is an engaging little plant growing in a tuft of crowded, narrow leaves of grey-green. The flowers of bright yellow are small, 1in. April/May.

ANTENNARIA

A. dioica 'Minima' forms a dense mat of spoon-shaped silvery-grey leaves and bears tight clusters of soft pink 'everlasting' flowers, 2in. May/June.

ARENARIA (Sandwort)

A. balearica grows flat on the ground. The leaves are minute and a very bright green, delicately fragrant. It is covered with tiny pure white upturned flowers on 1in stems in April/May. Although a rapid grower it is easily controlled as the roots are very fine and close to the surface. It should never be allowed to encroach upon slow-growing plants, but is excellent for covering a space where bulbs are dormant.

A. tetraquetra grows in a dense cushion of short-stemmed, closely overlapping little leaves terminating in small white flowers. June/July. It is very slow-growing and the quaint foliage is more attractive than the flowers.

ARTEMISIA

A. splendens 'Brachyphylla' is an invaluable foliage plant with finely cut leaves like lustrous silver lace, 1in. The flowers, which rise above the foliage, are a dull pale grey and if they are cut back the foliage becomes more dense and attractive; a splendid contrast with brightly coloured flowers.

ASPERULA (Woodruff)

A. gussonii forms a neat hummock of bright green short leaves growing in whorls on semi-prostrate stems. The tubular flowers of delicate pink are borne in terminal clusters, 1in to 2in. May/June.

A. suberosa has trailing stems of pale grey-green, ringed at regular intervals with short leaves of the same colour. The terminal clusters of flowers are small slender tubes opening out to four lobes of the palest pink. This enchanting plant is quite hardy in spite of its fragile appearance. April/July.

ASPLENIUM

A. ruta-muraria (Wall Rue) (fig 25) is one of the smallest ferns, with rather thick dark green fronds divided into wedge-shaped segments. In a sheltered position some of the fronds will last

Fig 25   *Asplenium ruta-muraria*

through the winter, but the new spring fronds are more attractive. 2in to 3in.

A. trichomanes (Maidenhair Spleenwort). A slender fern with finely divided fronds and stiff mid-rib of black or purplish brown. In winter some of the older pinnae die off, leaving the stiff black mid-ribs which spoil the appearance of the plant. These should be cut away to show the new young fronds. 2in to 4in.

Both these small ferns can be found growing in crevices in old stone walls, but it is not easy to induce collected ferns to grow if we try to reproduce the same conditions (ie apparently nothing to sustain them but old mortar rubble). So it is advisable to obtain a well-grown plant from a specialist nursery, rather than risk one taken from a wall crevice.

ASTILBE

A. glaberrima 'Saxosa' (fig 16) has dark bronze-green finely divided leaves and spikes of small fluffy rose-pink flowers, 4in.

109

June/July. Like the full-scale astilbes this is an excellent plant for a moist position in peaty soil beside a pool.

CALCEOLARIA

C. tenella (fig 26) is a quaint little plant with prostrate creeping stems and pale green leaves; the typical 'slipper' flowers are bright yellow on 2in stems. June/August. It does best in peaty soil in semi-shade; in some districts it has not proved hardy, but is well worth sheltering through a severe winter.

Fig 26   *Calceolaria tenella*

CAMPANULA

The number of species and hybrids is vast. Some are easy, but too large or too invasive for trough gardens; others are difficult to grow or to obtain. Between these two extremes there are many which are most desirable for the miniature garden. A few of the best which are not fussy about conditions and are available at most specialist nurseries are listed below.

C. arvatica is one of the neatest and prettiest; it will run freely and increase steadily in gritty soil and a sunny position.

forming a mat of light green foliage. The vivid purple flowers are wide upturned bells on slender stems, 1in to 2in. June/ July.

C. *arvatica* 'Alba', the white variety, is equally charming and shows to advantage when grown beside the above. Unfortunately, neither of them is a long-lived plant.

C. *cochlearifolia* (fig 27) (Syn: C. *pusilla*) is one of the easiest and most generous of this large family. It runs freely, winding its way between rocks and crevices, with light green, heart-shaped notched leaves. Numerous thin wiry stems rise up carrying two to six nodding bell flowers of purple. June/ August. There are several different forms, some pale lavender and others rich violet, and the white, C. *cochlearifolia* 'Alba'. 2in to 4in.

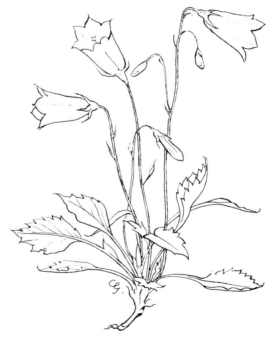

Fig 27   *Campanula cochlearifolia*

Fig 28   *Campanula hederacea*

C. hederacea (Syn: *Wahlenbergia hederacea*) the Ivy-leaved Campanula (fig 28) has slender trailing stems and leaves of pale green, forming a close mat when well established. In July/August minute, upturned exquisite little bell flowers of white suffused with blue rise up on hair-like stems, 1in above the foliage. A plant of ethereal beauty when grown in a position where it has plenty of moisture with good drainage.

C. x 'Norman Grove' is similar in habit to *C. cochlearifolia* but the flowers of rosy-lilac are not quite so pendulous. 3in to 4in. July/August.

C. pulla is one of the most striking of the bell flowers. The single nodding flowers are a rich dark purple. It is similar to the above, but not so rapid in growth and therefore more suitable for the smaller garden. 3in. July/August.

CENTAURIUM

C. portense (Syn: *C. scilloides*; *Erythraea chloodes*) is a neat little plant of the gentian family which bears bright pink flowers of a waxen texture all the summer. 2in to 3in. Once established, self-sown seedlings appear prolifically.

112

CRASSULA

C. cooperi (Syn: *C. bolusii*) is a very small succulent with speckled leaves varying from pale green to dark red; the tiny flowers are borne in clusters, deep pink in the bud, opening out white. Autumn. 1in to 2in. It is not hardy so needs a sheltered position and is admirable for indoor culture.

DIANTHUS

This is a very large genus including many with a neat compact habit, which makes them valuable for miniature gardens. Most of them grow in hummocks of slender grey-green foliage, with fragrant flowers.

D. alpinus bears single flowers of deep rose pink, speckled with a darker colour in the centre. 3in. May/July.

D. x 'Bella' is a compact little plant with small rich pink flowers; semi-double, with slightly serrated petals. 3in. June/July.

D. gratianopolitanus, popularly known as the Cheddar Pink, which used to be known as *D. caesius,* has grey foliage and bright pink flowers. 3in to 4in. May/July.

D. musalae is smaller than the above, growing in a compact tuft of silvery-green foliage with flowers of rich pink. 1in to 2in. June/July. A most engaging plant which is very slow-growing and should be protected from any which are invasive.

D. myrtinervis is quite unlike the others mentioned here. It forms a mat of fine trailing stems covered with small dark green leaves and terminal sprays of two or three minute flowers of vivid pink. This plant flowers generously all the summer and has great charm.

D. subacaulis is one of the neatest and most beautiful of this group. It grows in a compact hummock of slender leaves, with pale pink flowers. 1in to 2in. June/August.

DRABA (Whitlow Grass)

There are several drabas, small in leaf, bud and flower, admirable for the garden of limited dimensions.

113

D. aizoides forms a crowded tuft of light green stemless leaves with clusters of buttercup-yellow flowers on erect 2in stems. March / April.

D. bryoides grows in dense cushions of small moss-like foliage, which is more compact than the above. The golden yellow flowers, on hair-like stems, stand 2in above the foliage. March / April.

D. bryoides 'Imbricata' is similar to the above, but is even smaller and more compact. The foliage tends to go brown in winter and looks dead, but in spring the new growth is a vivid green; the flowers bright yellow. 1in. March / April.

EDRAIANTHUS (Syn : Wahlenbergia)
E. pumilio is a lovely plant which grows in neat tufts of slender silvery-grey leaves and bears numerous upturned bell flowers of very rich purple on short stems. In a light gritty soil and sunny position it flowers generously. 1in to 2in. May / June.

ERINUS
A gay little plant, delightful in trough gardens, between rocks or in the formal miniature garden in flowerbeds or borders. It is happy in sun or shade and seeds itself freely.

E. alpinus grows low on the ground in rosettes of wedge-shaped leaves with toothed margins. The flower stalks, 2in to 3in bear a profusion of small purple flowers at rather irregular intervals. May / July.

E. alpinus 'Albus' has pure white flowers; a good contrast with the above. *E.* 'Dr Hanele' has flowers of rich magenta, and *E.* 'Mrs C. Boyle' slightly larger flowers of glowing pink.

ERODIUM
E. chamaedryoides 'Roseum' grows in a flattish rosette of rounded scalloped leaves on a sturdy rootstock. Slender stalks carry single upturned flowers of pink, with streaks of deep rose colour, in profusion all the summer. 1in. A very good-

tempered plant which grows happily in sun or shade, but it is not entirely hardy in all districts and needs a sheltered position.

FRANKENIA (Sea Heath)

F. laevis (fig 29) is a prostrate plant which forms a mat of fine heather-like foliage which turns bronze or crimson in the autumn. In June to August it is covered with tiny stemless flowers of pale pink. A good plant to overhang the sides of a trough or to train over an arch.

Fig 29 *Frankenia laevis*

GENTIANA

G. verna 'Angulosa' is, when in flower, one of the most arresting and exquisite of all alpines (fig 30). The smooth leaves are broad, but pointed at the tips. The flower stalks carry very small leaves in pairs below the calyx; the flower, of gorgeous blue, is funnel-shaped with five widely spaced lobes, in the late spring. Once planted in an open sunny position they should not be disturbed and a group in bloom show a patch of colour which is never forgotten. A top-dressing of peaty soil is beneficial after flowering. It is not usually a long-lived plant, but even for a few seasons it is well worth growing to see this wondrous blue. It sets seeds generously to compensate for the short life. 2in to 3in.

Fig 30 *Gentiana verna* 'Angulosa'

GLOBULARIA

G. bellidifolia grows in dense hummocks of small dark green leaves; the pretty 'pom-pom' flowers of Wedgwood blue are carried singly on sturdy stalks. 2in to 3in. May/June.

GYPSOPHILA

G. fratensis grows in trailing sprays clothed with small grey-green leaves, and open clusters of tiny pale pink flowers rise on slender stems 2in to 3in above the foliage. May/July. An excellent plant to overhang the sides of a trough, where it remains smaller and more compact than in the open ground, but even so it must be controlled.

HELIANTHEMUM (Sun Rose)

H. alpestre 'Serpyllifolium' is a prostrate plant with trailing stems and small grey-green leaves bearing a profusion of gay little flowers of bright yellow. 1in. Summer.

H. oblongatum is similar to the above, but the leaves are dark green and glossy and the stems reddish. It also bears a profusion of small yellow flowers in the summer.

116

HELICHRYSUM

H. bellidioides 'Prostratum' forms a mat of slender much-branched stems with small dark green leaves, which are almost white on the under-surface, and terminal sprays of little white 'everlasting' papery flowers. 1in. May / June.

H. milfordae (*H. marginatum*) has low-growing rosettes of silver foliage. The fully-double flowers are white, with the outer petals flushed pink to bronze-red and are of the papery texture characteristic of 'everlasting' flowers. 2in to 3in. May / June.

HELXINE

H. soleirolii 'Golden Queen' is a flat carpeting plant with small round leaves of brilliant yellow. The flowers are inconspicuous; it is for the bright foliage that this plant is grown. It is not so invasive as the green form used on greenhouse staging, but it does grow fairly quickly and must be prevented from invading other plants. It is not hardy and is soon blackened by frost, but is an admirable plant for indoor culture where its glowing colour is so valuable.

H. soleirolii 'Silver Queen' is of the same habit, but the leaves are the palest silvery-green with creamy-white margins. It looks well in contrast with the above.

HOUSTONIA (Bluets)

H. caerulea 'Fred Millard' grows in clusters of small leaves close to the ground. The upturned four-pointed flowers of milky white suffused with blue are borne singly on hair-like stems 2in to 3in. May / July. A most engaging plant if grown in the right conditions which are shade, or semi-shade, in moist peaty soil. It will not tolerate hot sun or dry soil and is best in semi-bog conditions beside a pool.

HYPERICUM (St John's Wort)

H. anagalloides has trailing stems which radiate from a central crown, with pale green leaves and flowers of bright yellow (1in)

117

all the summer. A plant which thrives in almost any position and seeds itself freely.

H. empetrifolium 'Prostratum' forms a mat of heathery foliage and bears a profusion of gay yellow flowers. A splendid plant for a sunny position, overhanging a rock or the side of a trough. 1in to 2in. July / August.

H. trichocaulon has slender stems and light green leaves; the flower buds are bronze and the fully open flowers are bright yellow, the outer surface of the petals tinged with bronze. A very colourful plant when both bud and open flowers show simultaneously. If the dead flowers are cut off it will continue to bloom all the summer. 2in to 3in.

HYPSELLA

H. longiflora (Syn: *Selliera radicans*) has a creeping underground stem which sends down roots at frequent intervals; the smooth, dark green stemless leaves grow in pairs. The flowers are unusual and lovely, with five white petals suffused with pink; the three lower petals have streaks of crimson.

Fig 31   *Iris lacustris*

This is an endearing plant for crevices and it will wind its way between rocks, or mingle happily with campanulas and plants of similar habit but should not be allowed to invade choice cushion plants. 1in. All summer.

IRIS
I. lacustris (fig 31) is a captivating little iris with rhizome, leaves and flowers, all characteristic in form of the large 'flag' iris. The flowers, of transient beauty, are pale lilac; the 'falls' of the same colour have bold patches of rich violet and yellow. It does well in a sunny position. 3in to 4in. May/June and often again in the late summer.

LAURENTIA
L. tenella is a tiny plant which grows in rosettes of spathulate leaves. The five-petalled flowers are pale lilac with violet markings, truly minute, carried singly on 1in to 2in stems. All summer. A good plant for the smallest garden. It seeds itself freely, but can easily be weeded out if it is too prolific.

LINARIA (Toadflax)
L. alpina is semi-prostrate, with trailing stems radiating from the crown. The slender grey-green leaves grow at regular intervals along the stems, which have terminal sprays of tiny 'snapdragon' flowers of purple with glowing orange markings on the lip.

L. alpina 'Rosea' is a pink form.

L. faucicola is similar to *L. alpina*, but without the orange markings.

L. globosa 'Alba' is tufted in habit, with rounded leaves and pretty flowers of pure white with striking golden markings on the lip. 2in to 3in. Summer.

LINNAEA (Twin Flower)
L. borealis (fig 32) has creeping stems which lie close to the ground; the rounded leaves – some heart-shaped – have very

Fig 32 *Linnaea borealis*

short stalks. The slender bell-shaped flowers swing gracefully in pairs – back to back – on short stems which merge into one erect stalk, in a Y-shape, hence the name 'Twin Flower'. The bells of palest pink are five-lobed, with markings of rich crimson inside the tube. They are exquisitely beautiful and fragrant. A most desirable plant, which requires a good peaty soil in shade. The trailing stems can be encouraged to wind round and round within a limited area or, if space permits, allowed to wander at will. 2in. May / June.

LINUM
L. salsoloides 'Nanum' has semi-prostrate branchlets, ascending from a woody base covered with tiny grey-green leaves. The upturned, typical flax flowers are a pearly-white, crinkled and faintly flushed with bronze-purple on the reverse of the petals. A good plant for the side of a trough or close to a rock in a sunny position. 2in to 3in. May / June.

120

MENTHA (Mint)

M. requienii grows flat on the ground, the creeping stems covered with tiny rounded leaves which have a strong peppermint scent. It is sprinkled with microscopic stemless flowers of lilac colour in July to August. It is not long-lived, but usually produces many self-sown seedlings.

MESEMBRYANTHEMUM

M. ornatulum is a miniature form of the plant which is often used in bedding out in parks and seaside gardens. The stems are prostrate, the leaves fleshy; the fringed flowers are a brilliant magenta with a satiny sheen. 2in to 3in. All the summer. They are not hardy, but easily raised from seed.

MIMULUS

M. primuloides (fig 33) is a delightful miniature form of the

Fig 33 *Mimulus primuloides*

Musk flower, with low-growing foliage of bronze-green and has engaging little flowers of golden-yellow, borne singly on slender erect stems. 3in. June/August. It grows best in peaty soil, but good drainage is essential. The foliage dies down in winter, but new growth appears in the late spring.

MORISEA

M. monantha (Syn: *M. hypogaea*) grows in flat rosettes of dark green narrow leaves, which are deeply notched, somewhat fern-like in effect; the golden-yellow flowers on very short stems appear in May to June. A good plant for a sunny position, but it needs a minimum of 4in depth of soil and is one of the few plants which will not flourish in a very shallow trough.

MYOSOTIS

M. rupicola is a diminutive Forget-me-not, which bears clusters of sky-blue flowers 2in to 3in. May/June. It usually dies down in the winter and may not survive a severe season, but it can be propagated from seed and is well worth growing for its old-world charm.

NERTERA (Bead Plant; Fruiting Duckweed)

N. granadensis (Syn: *N. depressa*) has trailing stems, flat on the ground with tiny rounded leaves. The flowers are inconspicuous and, until the vivid orange berries appear in the early summer, it looks more like the common green helxine. In Victorian times it was grown in vast numbers for bedding out, but in these days it is rather scarce, which is sad as it is so attractive when sprinkled with the brilliant orange berries, like gleaming beads.

OXALIS

O. chrysantha has creeping stems which wind their way between rocks, small clover-like leaves, a wealth of goblet-shaped flowers of bright yellow, borne singly. 3in. Summer.

A pretty plant for a sunny position; it may become invasive, but is easily controlled as it is surface-rooting. Also, it is sometimes cut back by frost.

O. enneaphylla 'Minuta' has round glaucous leaves made up of nine or more pleated leaflets in a ruff-like effect. The pink funnel-shaped flowers have a pearly lustre. 1in to 2in. Summer.

O. lobata is a rare little treasure, very small and compact. The spring foliage rises about 1in from the tiny bulbils, but sometimes to the alarm and despair of the owner dies down again within a few weeks, but is only dormant. If watered, fresh foliage appears in the late summer, followed by the most exquisite goblet flowers of rich glowing gold with the outer petals suffused with flame colour. 2in. They are only fully open in sun and warm weather, folding back neatly in the cooler part of the day, to unfurl again the next day. When dormant the bulbils must be protected from excessive wet to prevent rot.

PARONYCHIA

P. serpyllifolia has grey-green foliage on trailing stems which cling to the ground, sometimes rooting as they spread. The flowers are inconspicuous, but are surrounded by papery bracts which have a silvery sheen.

PENSTEMON

P. procerus var. 'Formosus' grows in loose rosettes of small oval leaves on short stems. The tubular flowers, with irregular lobes of a vivid blue with a sheen of purple, are borne in clusters of 3 to 7 on erect stems. 1in to 2in. May to June.

PETROCALLIS

P. pyrenaica (Syn: *Draba pyrenaica*) forms a low cushion of bright green small leaves. The almost stemless flowers are pale lilac and slightly fragrant. 1in. May to June. A gem for the smallest garden which should be protected from the invasive plants.

PHLOX

P. douglasii. These are only suitable for larger trough gardens where a spread of 9in to 12in is not out of proportion. They are colourful in May and June, but unlike most alpines not very attractive except when they are covered with fairly large lilac flowers. The variety 'Eva' is bright pink with a darker centre and 'May Snow' is a clear white. There are several other named varieties.

PIMELIA (Rice Plant)

P. coarctata is an interesting and decorative plant for trailing over a rock or the sides of a trough. The prostrate shrubby stems are densely covered with tiny grey-green leaves and clusters of small stemless white flowers in May, followed by gleaming white berries, which account for its popular name.

POLYGALA (Milkwort)

P. calcarea is an elegant little plant with low-growing foliage and terminal sprays of small flowers, which are quite fascinating when closely observed. They have two winged sepals and one upper petal of gentian blue, whilst the lower petal has a fringed crest of a paler colour. 2in. May/June.

Fig 34   *Primula clarkei*

POTENTILLA

P eriocarpa grows in a dense mat of grey-green leaves. The upturned bright yellow flowers are borne in profusion all the summer.

P. verna 'Pygmaea' has dark green foliage and golden-yellow flowers. 1in to 2in. Although the name suggests that it is a spring-flowering subject, it usually continues to flower in the summer.

PRIMULA

P. clarkei (fig 34) has dark green oval leaves, sometimes heart-shaped. The flowers, rich rosy pink with a white centre notched at the apex of the petals are borne singly. 2in. March/April.

P. frondosa has pale green leaves, powdered white on the under-surface. Clusters of rosy-lilac flowers rise up on 3in to 4in stems. May/June. A handsome but variable plant. In some gardens it remains neat and compact, but in rich peaty soil it may become larger in all its parts and out of proportion with the other plants.

P. scotica (fig 35) is one of the most enchanting of all

Fig 35 *Primula scotica*

miniature plants. It grows in rosettes of small grey-green leaves which, like the flower stems and the calyx, are covered with a film of white powder. The flowers, about $\frac{1}{4}$in across, are a vivid purple of a rich velvety texture, with a greenish-white ring in the centre. They are borne in clusters and although only 1in to 2in high, are quite arresting in their beauty. Usually quite hardy they are not long-lived, but as they come freely from seed it is possible to maintain a continuity. May / June.

P. warschenewskyana is sturdier than the above. The leaves are more oval than is usual with primulas; they are sharply pointed with serrated margins. The flowers of rich pink with a white centre are borne singly. $\frac{1}{2}$in to 1in high. March / April.

RAOULIA

Small carpeting plants which grow very close to the ground and should be protected from soil splash by small chippings or coarse sand around the foliage.

R. australis has small leaves only just above the ground of shining metallic silver and is quite spectacular, especially when planted to contrast with some brilliant colour. The tiny stemless flowers are creamy white; it is for the foliage that this plant is grown.

R. glabra has dark green minute leaves in rosettes, which grow flat on the ground. The tiny flowers are also creamy white and stemless. This is a good plant for shade or semi-shade, but somewhat invasive, so must be controlled.

R. lutescens is even smaller than the two above. The microscopic leaves of grey-green are stemless and so close together that they suggest a fine woven fabric, or even a film of paint. The minute flowers are a dull golden yellow and it is for the foliage that this plant is so valuable.

SAXIFRAGA

Of this vast family there are a number which are decorative, hardy and small enough for trough gardens.

S. aizoon 'Baldensis' grows in neat hummocks of little rosettes – about ¼in across – of silvery-grey foliage. A very adaptable plant as it can be broken up into individual plantlets to edge a path or to grow in a narrow gorge between rocks. The sprays of creamy-white flowers, 2in high, rise up in June.

The Kabschia group grow in neat domes of small grey-green foliage and flower generously in the early spring. A few of the best are listed below.

S. burseriana 'Gloria' which has pure white flowers borne singly on bronze stems, 2in to 3in. February/March.

S. burseriana 'Sulphurea' is rather smaller than the above and has flowers of primrose yellow also on reddish stems, most effective against the grey-green foliage. 2in to 3in. March/April.

S. x 'Cranbourne' has flowers of a rich rose pink. 1in. March/April.

S. x 'Faldonside' is similar to *S. burseriana* 'Sulphurea', but the petals are a lemon yellow. 2in to 3in. March/April.

S. x 'Jenkinsae' bears flowers of pale pink with a touch of a deeper colour in the centre. 2in to 3in. March/April.

S. oppositifolia 'Splendens' is quite distinct from the Kabschia group, growing in mats of dark green foliage with upturned stemless flowers of crimson-purple in the early spring. 1in. *S. oppositifolia* 'Alba' is a white form and *S. oppositifolia* 'Latina' has bright pink flowers.

SEDUM (Stonecrop)
In this large family there are only a few small enough for trough gardens; most of the others should be avoided. The following are all small, but tend to increase rapidly by self-sown seedlings.

S. acre 'Minor' is a small form of the common Wall Pepper, with bright yellow flowers. 1in to 2in. Summer.

S. anglicum is more compact than the above; the bright green leaves are tinged with red and the flowers white, flushed pink. 1in. Summer.

S. dasyphyllum has small fleshy leaves which vary from glaucous green to soft rosy pink, delightfully opalescent in effect. The flowers are white. 1in. Summer.

S. farinosum is one of the best with small fleshy leaves packed closely together, shading from silvery-grey to rose pink, covered with a fine white powder. White starry flowers. 2in. Summer.

S. hispanicum 'Aureum' has bright yellow foliage, sometimes suffused with pinkish-bronze. White flowers. 1in. Summer.

S. humifusum is a little gem for the smaller garden, with minute stemless fleshy leaves of pale green. The flowers are yellow. ½in to 1in. June/July. It is not entirely hardy and may need shelter in winter in some districts.

SELAGINELLA
Non-flowering, but beautiful foliage plants.

S. apus (Syn: *S. apoda*) grows in clusters of very small fan-shaped sprays like delicate lace of bright green. 1in.

S. helvetica is much more open and trailing in habit. In semi-shade a bright green, but bronze in full sun. 1in to 2in.

S. helvetica 'Aurea' is similar to the above with bright golden foliage. All three should be protected from frost.

SEMPERVIVUM (Houseleek)
Most of these succulent plants are too large for miniature gardens, but the following are small and decorative throughout the year.

S. allionii has rosettes of incurved pointed leaves of pale green. Flowers of greenish-white. 2in to 3in. Summer.

S. arachnoideum (Cobweb Houseleek) has small rosettes of pointed leaves tinged with red, covered with a fine white cobweb. A well-grown plant is a delight. The flowers are a soft rose red. 3in. Summer. There are several forms of this.

S. arenarium grows in small rosettes of pointed leaves which turn crimson at the tips. In a well-drained soil and a sunny position the whole plant turns crimson. The greenish-white flowers are infrequent. 2in to 3in. June/July.

SILENE

S. acaulis grows in a dense cushion of small, stemless pointed leaves and bears a profusion of upturned deep pink flowers resting on the foliage in June. 1in to 2in. There is a white variety, *S. acaulis* 'Alba'.

SOLDANELLA (Alpine Snowbell)

S. alpina, when happily established in semi-shade and peaty soil, is one of the most lovely of all alpines. The leaves are kidney-shaped and rather leathery. The nodding flowers of rosy-purple are bell-shaped and fringed, with a graceful outward curve. 2in to 3in. March/April.

S. minima (The Least Snowbell) is very much smaller, with slender tubular flowers of pale lilac shading to milky-white, also fringed. 2in. March/April.

S. montana (Mountain Tassel Flower) is slightly larger than *S. alpina* with rosy-lilac flowers, funnel-shaped and deeply fringed. 4in to 6in. March/April.

THALICTRUM

T. kiusianum is a plant of subtle charm, somewhat like a Maidenhair Fern. The flowers of small fluffy rosy-lilac clusters are erect. 3in to 4in. Spring.

THYMUS

T. serpyllum 'Minimus' is a small form of the wild thyme, with tiny dark green leaves on flat trailing stems and minute lilac-coloured flowers. ½in. June/July. A fragrant plant which is excellent to overhang the sides of a trough, but it should not be allowed to invade other plants.

VERONICA

V. rupestris 'Nana' (Syn: *V. prostrata*) has trailing stems with very dark green leaves, terminating in spikes of gentian blue flowers. 3in. May/July. There is a pink form, *V. rupestris* 'Rosea' of similar habit.

VIOLA

V. hederacea (Syn: *Erpetion reniforme*). (Australian Violet). Creeping stems and pale green ivy-shaped leaves. The flowers are characteristic of the violet, but smaller; deep purple in the centre shading off to white on slender 2in stems. May/September or later. A lovely plant for a sheltered position.

V. yakusimana is so minute and yet so perfectly proportioned that it is almost unbelievable. The tiny leaves are heart-shaped and the flowers white with markings of rich purple. This is a treasure, deserving a special position and protection from invasive plants. 1in. Summer.

WAHLENBERGIA

W. saxicola (Syn: W. tasmanica). A creeping plant related to the campanulas and of similar habit, with narrow spoon-shaped leaves of light green and slender bell flowers of lilac blue, shading to milky-white, borne singly on 2in stems. July/October.

Bulbs

FRITILLARIA

F. citrina is a most captivating little plant with grey-green leaves and single flowers of citrus yellow which swing gracefully on 4in stems. The outer petals turn back in a beautiful curve which makes this a plant of unique elegance. March/April.

NARCISSUS

There are several miniature daffodils small enough for trough gardens.

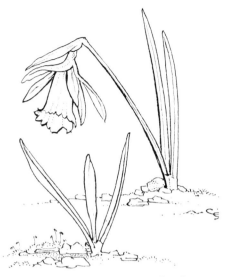

Fig 36   *Narcissus asturiensis*

N. asturiensis (Syn: *N. minimus*) is a perfect little yellow trumpet daffodil (fig 36). 2in to 3in. January/February.

N. cyclamineus has a slender yellow trumpet and reflexed petals of the same colour. 3in to 4in. March/April.

N. juncifolius has clusters of three or four short trumpet flowers of bright yellow which are sweetly scented. 3in to 4in. March/April.

RHODOHYPOXIS

R. baurii is one of the few bulbous plants which flower in the late spring and summer. The leaves are slender, grey-green; the flowers, of a velvety texture, are the most arresting cerise pink. 2in. After flowering, as the leaves die down, their position should be marked so that the tiny bulbils are not disturbed whilst dormant. There are several named varieties in different shades of pink, red and also a white form, *R. platypetala*.

SCILLA

S. verna is a rare little bulb – not as well known as it should be – much smaller than other scillas. Slender dark green leaves and very pretty pale violet flowers with numerous stamens of a richer colour. 3in. April/May.

Annuals

IONOPSIDIUM

I. acaule (Violet Cress) is a tiny plant which flowers profusely. The name is misleading as the flowers are usually pale lilac, almost white in a sunny position. Unlike most annuals it continues producing seedlings throughout the year, even through ice and snow. 1in to 1½in.

Fig 37 *Sedum coeruleum*

SEDUM

S. coeruleum (fig 37) has succulent leaves of pale green which turn bronze-red in summer, when it is covered with myriads of tiny flowers of sky blue. As most sedums have yellow or white flowers this is an unusual and valuable plant for colour in the late summer.

Aquatics

A pool only a few inches across can have some floating plants. There should be a layer of small pebbles at the base of the container – which must be watertight – and a layer of sieved soil mixed with a few pieces of charcoal. Water should be poured in gently and allowed to settle before adding the plants.

AZOLLA

A. caroliniana (Fairy Moss) is a minute floating plant, fern-like in appearance, making an attractive pattern on the water. It is blue-green in the spring, turning to bronze-red in the autumn.

HYDROCHARIS

H. morsus-ranae (Frogbit) has kidney-shaped leaves about 1in across, which float on the surface and the three-petalled white flowers rise just above the water in summer. In the autumn, little buds for next season's growth drop into the mud to reappear in the late spring.

After a while a pool may need a little attention; any dust on the surface should be skimmed off and, if necessary, extra water added to compensate for evaporation. Algae, known as blanket weed (which looks like a mass of slimy green threads), may grow in the water and this must be removed. If the azolla or hydrocharis become entangled in it, the best thing is to put them in a bowl of clean water and make sure the pool is clear of the weed before replacing the plants.

———

Space does not allow a more extensive list with descriptions of trees and plants, but the reader can, by visiting various nurseries, find some of those mentioned in this book as well as other plants which are suitable for growing in troughs. It may be necessary to select from different nurseries, for if there is no demand some specialist nurseries cease to grow a few of the more unusual alpines.

Apart from the pleasure these plants will give the owner,

there would be the additional satisfaction that by growing some of the more uncommon plants they will keep up a demand for some quite enchanting species which are not as well known as they should be and so contribute to conservation.

Author's Note

Readers who wish to have further information about miniature trees, plants and gardens can write (enclosing a stamped and addressed envelope) to the author at Chignal-Smealey, Chelmsford, Essex.